IraqiGirl

TUESDAY, NOVEMBER 16TH, 2004

It is impossible to imagine what the Iraqi feels right now

Do you know that Aya's grandfather was killed last Thursday by one of the American soldiers' bullets? When Aya is eight years old and asks me how her grandfather died, what will I answer her? What do you think I should answer her? When I tell her the American soldiers killed him, of course she will ask me why and how and did I do anything about that?

The answer to her question is this post and the others. I can answer her that I did do something about it. I did what I could in that time. I wrote in my blog about what is going on in Iraq.

IraqiGirl

Diary of a Teenage Girl in Iraq

Edited by Elizabeth Wrigley-Field
Developed by John Ross

Haymarket Books
Chicago, Illinois

First published in 2009 by Haymarket Books
©2009 Haymarket Books

P.O. Box 180165
Chicago, IL 60618
773-583-7884
info@haymarketbooks.org
www.haymarketbooks.org

Trade distribution:
In the U.S. through Consortium Book Sales, www.cbsd.com
In the UK, Turnaround Publisher Services, www.turnaround-psl.com
In Australia, Palgrave MacMillan, www.palgravemacmillan.com.au
In all other countries, Publishers Group Worldwide, www.pgw.com

This book was published with the generous support of the Wallace Global Fund.

Cover design by Amy Balkin

ISBN: 978-1931859-73-8

Printed in Canada by union labor on recycled paper containing 100 percent post-
consumer waste in accordance with the guidelines of the Green Press Initiative,
www.greenpressinitiative.org.

Library of Congress CIP Data is available

10 9 8 7 6 5 4 3 2 1

CONTENTS

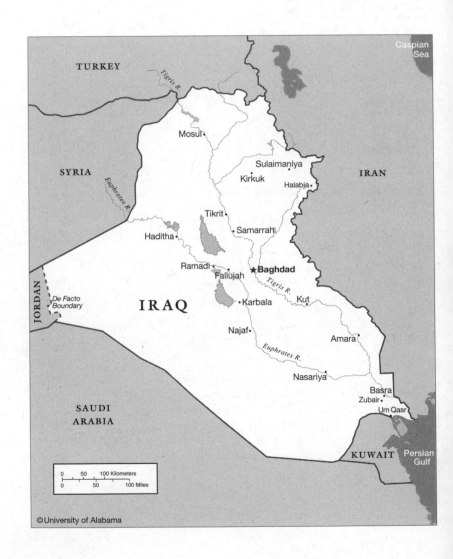

TURKEY

Caspian
Sea

Tigris R.

Mosul

SYRIA

Sulaimaniya

Kirkuk

Halabja

IRAN

Euphrates R.

Tikrit

Haditha

Samarrah

Ramadi

Fallujah

★Baghdad

Tigris R.

JORDAN

De Facto
Boundary

IRAQ

Karbala

Kut

Najaf

Amara

Euphrates R.

Nasariya

Basra

SAUDI
ARABIA

Zubair

Um Qasr

KUWAIT

Persian
Gulf

| 0 | 50 | 100 Kilometers |
| 0 | 50 | 100 Miles |

©University of Alabama

Coming of Age
Under U.S. Occupation
John Ross

The world marks the sixth year of the war in Iraq with no end in sight. Just as others in my generation could not remember a time when there was no Vietnam War, my life seems to have begun with the current massacre. What came before has been erased.

I was just a whippersnapper of sixty-five back then when in February 2003 I signed on with the Human Shields and rode up to Baghdad in a London double-decker bus to interpose my body between Bush's bombs and the Iraqi people. Most of us were sure we were going to die and we were prepared to pay the price to stop the war before it began. But we didn't die and we didn't stop the war. Six years later here I am, to my amazement, having turned seventy. The war, like my life, goes on. And on.

As the crude reality of imminent attack closed in on Iraq, Saddam Hussein flew a bunch of us Shields up to Mosul 240 miles north of

Baghdad during the first week of March 2003. Mosul is Iraq's largest Sunni majority city and with a population of 1.7 million, the nation's third largest city behind Baghdad and Basra. Despite the Sunni majority, Mosul has a lively ethnic mix. Bordered by Kurdistan, a substantial portion of the population wears the Kurdish colors. Turkmen, Christians, and Yazedis—the non-Muslim sect slaughtered by unknowns in August 2007—are all players in the ethnic push and pull. There are few Shias in Mosul.

Saddam Hussein rewarded the loyalty of Mosul's Sunnis by selecting many of his elite army officers from the city, and the now-outlawed Baath party ruled local politics. In the summer of 2003, Saddam Hussein's sons, Uday and Qusay, on the run from their American pursuers, sought refuge in Mosul, only to be taken out by U.S. sharpshooters when they were betrayed by a local.

Mosul, the capital of Nenevah province, a region celebrated for its many (now-looted) ruins, was a strategically sited city in the middle of the U.S.-imposed no-fly zone. Nenevah abuts Syria on the northwest and Turkey further north and it became a critical transit point for black market oil out of the country and for foreign fighters flocking in to join the resistance further south.

The Sunnis of Mosul bristled at the presence of U.S. troops, who encamped on the outskirts of town and often drew fire from the locals. Twenty-two American troops were killed when a suicide bomber entered their mess tents in December 2004.

The November 2004 U.S. push into Fallujah, just days after George W. Bush had been reelected president, triggered an uptick in fighting in Mosul as insurgents fleeing that western city moved north to Nenevah. U.S. convoys sent south from Mosul to join their comrades in Fallujah sometimes crossed paths with the rebels on the roads.

While the brutal battle for control of Fallujah raged, a similar battle was joined in Mosul. The militants seized whole districts, attacked police stations and prisons, and confronted Iraqi army patrols. U.S. troops we're poured back into the fray. Repeated curfews were declared.

The battle for Mosul has ebbed and flowed ever since, sometimes more intensely than in Baghdad. Every night, bodies are dumped in the neighborhoods on the banks of the Tigris River. Explosions and gunshots puncture the sleep of the citizenry. In 2007, as the Bush surge kicked in down-river in Baghdad, a fresh wave of insurgents converged on Mosul, compounding the daily violence.

Last year I lived in Mosul for months, without ever checking out of this cavernous hotel in the old quarter of Mexico City where I've been in residence for the past twenty-three years. In a book project begun in 2006, I've been collaborating with Hadiya, a spirited Iraqi teenager from Mosul, weaving together four years of blogging into a narrative.

Hadiya has indeed come of age during Bush's war in Mosul. When she began her blog in July 2004, she chatted up her Barbies and her bears and posted pictures of her pink room on the Internet. Then she retold the conversations between friends at school: one walks out her door to find a corpse in the street. "That's nothing," another school chum tells them, "there was a body without a head on my street."

Hadiya's life is fixated on family and school — school and studying provide a stabilizing space in the middle of the chaos of war. But sometimes when she gets to school, her classroom has been hit by a missile. Just getting to school can put her life and those of her family at risk. One day, her dad, a respected doctor in Mosul, was roughly pulled from his car by U.S. troops, forcibly searched and made to stand in the broiling sun for hours while Hadiya's sister and her sister's two-year-old daughter sat in the sweltering car. When the child began to cry, her mother was afraid to reach for the bottle of water in her purse because any movement could have caused the U.S. soldier standing by to shoot her.

Hadiya's relatives have been killed. Some have had to leave Iraq. Her beloved grandfather grew weary and died in May 2007. "Bomb cars" break out the kitchen window all the time but the family no longer replaces them. What's the use?

Hadiya's resentment at how Bush and his war have messed up her childhood is redemptive. "I'm sixteen. These should be the happiest years of my life. I should be a wild girl doing crazy foolish things," she complains, locked up one night after the next by the eternal curfews. "We go to sleep at 10 o'clock now like the chickens. Are we chickens?" she asks.

Black humor abounds. One day, her sister Najma narrowly escapes a car-bomb blast outside the university. When she returned home, as Hadiya tells it, Najma refuses to do housework. "I was going to die today and you want me to wash the dishes?" she demands of her mother. Anne Frank's ghost floats over the jokes Hadiya intersperses in the text.

The year of Bush's surge was a rough one for Hadiya, and for Mosul. The curfews keep her counting the walls ("there are still four in each room"), and she is terminally bored as only a teenager can be. Her college board exams were called off three times because of the war in Mosul. But there are pluses — "The sound of the American airplanes has helped this community to discover the value of silence."

Hadiya is pessimistic about the future. "Life is one thing we are not very good at," she writes, signing her post, "Your lost friend from where Iraq once was."

Yet she translates for us the experience of her generation, trapped in their homes and schools by the disasters of a war that has been imposed upon them by adult politics. Hadiya's fondest memories are of driving with her dad on starry Mosul nights to buy ice cream. For six years now, going out for ice cream can get her killed.

There are many Iraqi girls and boys, and this is the story of what they have lost in this war: their precious childhoods. Hadiya implores us never to let this tragedy happen again. Her book is a reminder that ending war is our most important homework.

John Ross
June 2009
Mexico City

Editor's Note

Hadiya began her blog just under a year and a half into the U.S. occupation of Iraq. She writes from Mosul, a diverse city with many Sunni Muslims, like Hadiya's family. Mosul has become one center of resistance to the occupation.

Hadiya's name is not really Hadiya. We have used pseudonyms for every Iraqi in this story because each of their lives could be in danger if they were identified. But Hadiya is a real teenager in Mosul, and this is her story.

My Life and My Country

JULY 29

About me and my life

I am a girl, fifteen years old. I have two sisters. I have a great father; he is a doctor, and a great mother who is an engineer. We live in Mosul, a city in the north of Iraq.

My grandfather is a scientist and a professor of engineering. He and my grandmother and my cousins and relatives live in Baghdad. We travel to see them every summer.

My big sister is married and I don't have a brother so I spend most of my time with my other sister Najma (talk, fight, cook, and laugh). She's really funny but we're different. I love what she hates, she hates what I love. All my friends look to me as lucky to have a sister like her and I think you would agree with them.

I feel that I am special. I look at life in a different way. I love life, I love people, and I wish the best for my family and my friends.

The hero of my childhood is my grandfather. He is a wonderful man. I can't describe it. I just saw him last week and I miss him already. I want to be like him.

Because I am the youngest, I look like Cinderella. Thank God for everything.

FRIDAY, JULY 30

My own room

I love that I have my own room because I can put this bear here and that doll here. I feel that my room represents me.

About my room: It is

pink and small and nice. It is near my sister Najma's room and that is a problem. But it is comfortable. I have a very big bed. I can move from the right side to the left side. The first day I slept in my bed I fell to the ground more than once. Najma said, "I heard *boom baaam boom baaam*."

I cleaned my room today and I found my copybook from the examination days last month. Thank God that they ended.

I love to decorate my room with bears and the things I love because that gives me back my memories.

Here you can see my small desk. I have story-books, history books, and poetry books. There are Islamic books too. I love to read.

A funny story for you: When I sleep, my eyes are nearly open and that scares people. When my aunts came to Mosul from Baghdad, they refused to sleep in the same room with me. One day when I was sleepy, my sister Najma told me: "Don't forget to close your eyes."

FRIDAY, AUGUST 13

Iraq's treasure

I live in a rich country. Iraq is one of the richest countries in the world. One of our treasures are the dates. We had twenty million date trees before the war. We were second to Saudi Arabia in the number of date trees.

Dates grow in the south of Iraq more than in the north because dates need heat and light to grow as well as water and humidity, which we have in the south of Iraq.

Dates are very useful to us. It is one of the fruits mentioned in the Holy Quraan and Muhammad, the Messenger of God, advises us to eat this fruit. In September, this fruit will ripen and will be available in all the markets of Iraq.

MONDAY, AUGUST 23
Surprise

Cream puffs. This is one of my favorite sweets. Yesterday when my mother went to the university and Najma was still asleep, I was thinking about what I could cook to surprise my mother. The first thing that came to my mind was cream puffs. But there was no electricity.

WEDNESDAY, AUGUST 25
Wishes and luck

Today I woke up when my big sister called. "Hadiya, Najma, it's nine o'clock. You should wake up. We are going out."

Thank God the bombing has stopped.

I went to the kitchen and ate breakfast with my mother and sister and then went upstairs and told Najma she should wake up now. Luckily, she didn't shout at me.

I changed my clothes quickly and when I went to open the door, I saw two children playing. I remembered myself when I was their age: what beautiful days we lived.

When we visited the hairdresser all the women were talking about the bombs and the soccer game we lost yesterday. I felt so sorry that we lost.

After that we went to the shop. Najma wanted to buy Pringles but I saw that they were made in the USA and not in the Arabian land. Why do we buy things made in the USA? We don't have to buy them.

On the trip back to our house we saw two white camels! I had never seen a white camel in my life and there it was! I saw a white butterfly in our garden too. I'm lucky today.

I have a wish: I should tell it to you. I want to tell everybody my wish and shout it as loud as I can. I want a real freedom. I want a real democracy. I want peace all over Iraq. No more fighting between Iraqi people. No more blood. Our oil is for building the new Iraq.

SATURDAY, SEPTEMBER 4
Aya

This is Aya, my sister's daughter. She was born September 1, 2004. I love this baby who doesn't let me sleep. Nice baby, huh???

MONDAY, SEPTEMBER 6
Mecca

This is Al-Kaaba's picture. It is our dream to go there, me and other Muslims. I hope my dream will come true and I ask God to go to Mecca before I die.

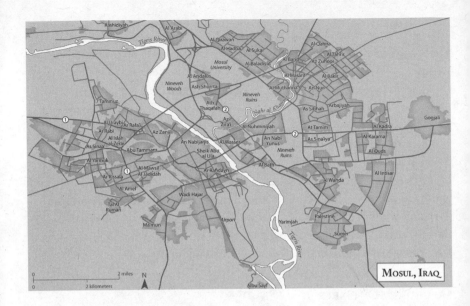

TUESDAY, SEPTEMBER 7

...and Mosul

Mosul is my city. It lies in the north of Iraq. The distance between Mosul and Baghdad is about 396 kilometers. Mosul was built on the fragments of Nenevah. It is the biggest city in the north and the third city in Iraq. Arabs are the people who live in Mosul and its history begins in 1080 BC when the Assyrians made it their capital and built walls around it.

FROM ANONYMOUS:

What I liked about Mosul is how many different people of various ethnic and religious groups seem to live together peacefully. I hope this never changes. Also the University of Mosul is an outstanding university. The best thing about Mosul, I think, is the children.

FROM HADIYA:

Thank you. Right, different people of various ethnic and religious groups seem to live together peacefully in Mosul, like me and my friend who is Christian but she is one of my best best friends. And the university in Mosul is one of the best universities in Iraq.

I also visit Baghdad every year. I still remember my last visit before the war. It was so beautiful, and I remember my mom told me, "Look at this like it's your last visit; we don't know what will happen, and after the war when we visit, Baghdad will still be nice, but never like it was before."

Fifteen Years Old in Occupied Iraq

Today

In the morning, Dad went to the hospital and Mom to the university and me and Najma and Aya stayed at home. We woke up when Aya started crying and never stopped. I began to prepare our lunch and to do something about Aya's crying. My mother came home and sang Aya her favorite song.

My big sister was so worried because her husband was coming to Mosul today or tomorrow and there was plenty of bombing here and in Baghdad. At one o'clock he called to tell her he was in Mosul now, so my sister took Aya home.

Then my dad called and told us he would be late because there was a bombing in the street and the streets were crowded.

We heard on TV about the killing of one of the reporters on Al-Arabiya. We had watched him on TV before he died. Then my mother's friend came to our house. She couldn't get to her house because of all the people crowded in the streets.

After all this news, I will try not to be sad. The good news is that my uncle is coming to Mosul and he'll stay with his family in our home. Inshallah. I hope that we will have a good time.

THURSDAY, OCTOBER 7

Back to school

Hello again. Bad news. School began last Saturday so we go to school every day now. The headmistress of our school gave me the oldest biology book. It was published in 1995. That means I was six years old when it was published! But the problem became worse.

When I got home, Najma was looking at my book and found that it was for her level. And then she took it from me because hers did not have all the pages.

Yesterday, my English teacher asked us what "onion" meant in Arabic and I answered "*zitoon*" (olive) and she said, "Wrong answer." When I got home, I told my mother and my sisters that the teacher had asked us what "onion" means in Arabic and Najma said loudly the answer was "zitoon." At that moment, I looked at her and said now I know where I got this wrong information.

In fact, I don't use a dictionary much because I have Najma. She is really a good dictionary. Usually.

TUESDAY, OCTOBER 19

Tired of bombs

I had a very bad day today. First, when we went to school we heard the sound of bombing nearby and I didn't do well in my exam. In the sixth lesson, we heard another bomb. My dad was near it but thank God he is OK. When we reached home, another bomb went off near my aunt's house and all her windows were broken and the door needs to be repaired because it's not opening anymore. After those three bombs came three more.

When I got home, Aya was not there. So the only thing I did was sleep and study. I'm tired.

MONDAY, OCTOBER 25

Can life get worse?

I had a physics examination and I think I did well on it. But I don't care about the exams the way I did before. There are plenty of things that I think about now, plenty of problems that I can't fix. Plenty of bad situations I can't change.

Do you ever feel that you are imprisoned in a cage and there is no one except you and a big lion in this cage and you can't get out? You can't get out and there is nowhere to run. No way to run. That is my feeling.

Every day I say that life can't get worse, but I find that it can. My friend told the girl who sits beside her that if she killed herself, no one would ask why.

I am sure that none of you could live one day in Iraq. In Iraq now there is no happy word in our dictionary. When I look at Aya, I hope that her future will be better than ours. But the question is do we have a future? I cry and cry but what will happen after that? I can't change the situation whether I cry or not.

As you know we are in the month of Ramadan and we don't have enough rest. Only yesterday, there were helicopters and they threw plenty of rockets and grenades in the same area where we were.

Ramadan is a monthlong Muslim holiday. During Ramadan, observant Muslims fast from dawn until sunset, and pray regularly. Those who are unable to fast, such as the elderly, may strive to feed the impoverished in place of fasting. The end of Ramadan is marked by the holiday Eid al-Fitr (Festival of Breaking the Fast), which may involve feasts, prayer, gifts to food to the poor, and visiting friends and relatives.

WEDNESDAY, NOVEMBER 3

Quiet, normal Iraq

Today was a normal day at school. I had an exam and I did OK. Then I had a French lesson and I couldn't understand what the teacher said. I was absent-minded all the time. I know that this is not good, but what can I do? I heard the sound of bombings and bullets and I couldn't concentrate.

When I say today was a quiet day, that doesn't mean there were no bullets or bombs. When I say today was a normal day, that doesn't mean there were no explosions—because if there were no bombs, then it would not be a normal day.

It is easy to learn English because my parents and my sisters can help me. But with French, nobody can help. I really have a problem with French. I can't pronounce anything correctly. And it's hard to write anything. There is one word that has twelve letters!

These days, I'm full of sadness. Every night I have a nightmare. My nightmare today was that our taxi driver who takes us to school every day kidnapped me and Najma and took us somewhere dark.

I will write to you again.

Wait for me.

SATURDAY, NOVEMBER 6

Day of my life

Here I am writing to you again in spite of the bad situation around me. On Tuesday when I heard that Bush won and the American soldiers will begin to attack Fallujah, I began to cry and couldn't stop. My head was aching so I went to bed without finishing my homework. But in the morning when we went to school, there was a checkpoint. That gave me a little moment to look in my books and study the information there.

When we were on the road to the school one of the girls who was in the taxi with us shouted, "Ohhhh, look at our school! It's not there!" We looked at her and wondered what she was talking about. It was not our school that was bombed, just one of the many buildings that the Americans have destroyed in this war. Sometimes, you feel that you are not in the same area where you lived all your life.

After school, we went to the shop to find clothes for me while Najma and my father went to the dentist. I was so tired and now my leg aches. There is a saying that if your leg aches, you will be tall. That's good.

SATURDAY, NOVEMBER 13

Dear America

Don't ask me any questions about what's happening in Mosul, because the situation is bad. Thank you, America, for your help. You have made my life more difficult than it was. Worse than it was. We are more scared now.

I should ask you a question: What do you do when someone enters your house without your permission? I mean, "Enters by force." Tell me what do you do?

I would be a liar if I told you I couldn't sleep last night because I was so sad. The truth is that I couldn't sleep because the Americans were bombarding our neighborhood. What should I say? I have so many words I want to write. But I can't.

Until when must we follow what America says? How long must we follow orders?

Who is America? Ha!

We have the oldest civilizations. We have oil. And we have the capability to rule ourselves.

I respect the American people who are not with this war. I respect the American people who love Iraq and want peace. I respect the American people my parents talk to me about—they lived in America twenty years ago and they admire the American people. But not the Americans who have come to Iraq now. Not them. My parents were surprised when they saw the character of the American soldiers.

Tomorrow is our holiday. It will be Eid al-Fitr. But because of your help, I will stay home and not go anywhere all day. You know why, of course. If you don't offer your help tomorrow, it could be one of the best days of my life.

But you help me. You help everybody in the world to destroy their own countries.

But believe me, it is time to help yourself.

MONDAY, NOVEMBER 15

Talking about me

Someone asked me to put pictures of Mosul on the blog. I want to tell him that I would love to do this, but how can I take a picture if I can't leave my house?

I received many comments and letters saying that I am not Iraqi. Another one said that I don't deserve the freedom that the Americans are bringing to the Iraqi people. That my view of the war is wrong and I should change it. I'll tell you what—no one in this world can know what I am feeling.

I respect your view of the American soldiers, but it is not you who is prevented from sleeping by the sound of bullets. It is not you who every day is woken up by the sound of bombs. It is not you who hears the rocket falling and doesn't  know if it will be on his house or his aunt's house or his grandfather's. It is not you who saw tanks and many American soldiers in front of his house. And it is not you who the American soldiers prevent from leaving their own home and if you do, they will simply kill you.

It is not you who heard the bullets and looked out of the window and saw that the Americans were moving in and the car door was open and there was blood on the ground of the street and you want to go out and help the driver because you know he is wounded and needs your help.

I'll tell you what. I don't like my life. But at least I am a human and I have feelings and I am a free person. Let me remember this poem that says:

Am I free and unrestrained?
Or do I walk in chains?
Do I lead myself in this life?
Or am I being led?
Am I the one who is walking on the road?
Or is this the road that is moving?
Or are we both standing still
And is it time that is running?
I wish I knew
But I don't know.

Do you love your baby?

هل تحب طفلك ؟

We do also.

ونحن أيضا

Do you protect him?

هل تستطيع أن تحميه؟

We can't.

نحن لا نستطيع

Do you like their smile?

هل تحب ضحكتهم؟

Me too.

وأنا أيضاً

Do you like peace?

هل تحب السلام ؟؟

Everyone likes peace...

الكــل يحب السلام

Do you like freedom?

هل تحب الحـــرية؟

Everyone loves freedom.

الكل يحب الحرية

TUESDAY, NOVEMBER 16

It is impossible to imagine
what the Iraqi feels right now

Do you know that Aya's grandfather was killed last Thursday by one of the American soldier's bullets? When Aya is eight years old and asks me how her grandfather died, what will I answer her? What do you think I should answer her? When I tell her the American soldiers killed him, of course she will ask me why and how and did I do anything about that.

The answer to her question is this post and the others. I can answer her that I did do something about it. I did what I could in that time. I wrote in my blog about what is going on in Iraq. How the American soldiers attack Iraq.

Yesterday I could walk outside but a few meters from the door of our home; we met an American soldier. At that moment, I felt that one of two things could have happened: (1) he killed me or (2) I killed him.

I feel sick today. This is the third day of Eid al-Fitr but I don't feel we are in Eid yet. We have not been able to leave our home except for yesterday to visit my aunt's house, which is not far away.

MONDAY, NOVEMBER 17

I have an announcement

Because I am fifteen years old and I haven't traveled to any place like you and I don't know what the people around the world are thinking, I don't have enough experience. But because I am an Iraqi girl, I am not one of those people who don't know what is going on around them. Everybody in Iraq has their view of the war and the American soldiers and Saddam.

I read all the comments that you wrote. Some of them hurt me. Some of them made me nervous. Some of them made me cry. I don't know if I should believe you or not. I know that you are looking out for my happiness and you wish the best for me. But I am really tired. In fact, I don't understand what you wrote.

My father advised me not to write about political situations. That's because I am still young. So I will change the kind of subject that I write about.

Dear Hadiya,

I am not going to lecture or preach to you. All I can say is I am sorry for what you and other innocent Iraqis are going through. I am an army wife whose husband is in Iraq for the second time in less than two years. But I don't pretend to know what it's like to walk in your shoes. I just wish for peace.

MONDAY, NOVEMBER 22

How it happened

Someone asked me how I could be sure that Aya's grandfather was killed by the bullets of an American soldier's gun?

Here is my answer.

When Aya's grandfather was killed, he was with one of his neighbors. They were walking back home because at the time there was a lot of shooting in the area and the Americans closed the roads leading to their house. The place where he got shot was an open area and there were no shelter to protect them from fire.

There was a shop nearby and the shop owner invited them to enter his place until the shooting stopped. But Aya's grandfather refused, probably because he was worried about his family. So he continued to walk.

In front of Aya's grandfather on the way to his home about one hundred meters away, there was an American Stryker vehicle. The American soldiers who were in that Stryker shot him in the thigh. The bullet caused severe bleeding and he fell to the ground.

His neighbor and the shopkeeper tried to take Aya's grandfather to the shop but the American soldier shot them too. This happened every time they tried to bring him to a safe place to stop the bleeding. When the shooting calmed down, they were able to take him to a safe place and put a bandage over the wound. But they couldn't find a car to take Aya's grandfather to the hospital in time and he died on the way from the bleeding. In the hospital, they told the family that the bullet had cut his "femoral artery."

THURSDAY, NOVEMBER 25

No more

I was talking with my friend by e-mail and I decided I wouldn't comment anymore about the war in my blog.

Today is like every day in Iraq. No electricity, no fun, and no peace. Just explosions, destruction, and "accidental killings."

Believe me, I haven't gone out of the house for a long time. But that's OK—there is good news. "Maybe I can go to school next week."

Now after thirty-four hours without electricity, I feel cold. The winter came on suddenly. I think our school will be cold if we go back on Saturday.

The best thing is that your family is always with you and supporting you in your life. When I come home from school I am tired but when I see my family I feel better and my face changes from a sad face to a happy one. I don't know why I don't just write about my family.

Yesterday I was so sad and I don't know how my uncle knew about that. He talked to me like a brother not like an uncle. But I don't know how a brother talks to his sisters because I don't have any brothers. Do your brothers talk to you like your sisters do? Is there a difference?

Goodbye now and see you later.

Curfew over

Today we went to school after seventeen days of staying at home. I saw my friends and they are good, but they felt sad like I do and they didn't stop telling me scary stories of things that happened in the past few weeks....

THURSDAY, DECEMBER 9

Sleeping, not sleeping, and waking up

Hello everybody.

I am so busy with the examinations this week. I did well on them but not as well as I should. My sadness increases from day to day. I don't have enough time to sleep, just seven or six hours. And I don't have a good time when I sleep because of the nightmares.

But on the other hand, I feel that I have been sleeping all my life and now I have woken up and opened my eyes to the world. A beautiful world!! But impossible to live in.

I know I should do something for my country but I don't know what it is and how I can do it alone without any help FROM THE IRAQI PEOPLE. There is a saying that you can't clap with just one hand. So I'm wondering what I should do.

My friend was so upset the past few days because there were plenty of explosions near her house and all her windows were broken. Another girl came to the class and started talking about what happened near her home and she said the Americans destroyed the mosque in her neighborhood. They were both sad.

About the exams. We had three examinations today. While we were writing the answers in our books, we heard a big bomb. And because there were so many bombs and bullets, the headmaster of the school told us that we should be in school at 8 o'clock but that we would go back home by 12:15.

I don't want to share my feelings this week because I don't feel good so I will stop now.

THURSDAY, DECEMBER 18

Long days

I didn't do well on my examination. I don't know what happened to me...I can't believe that it was me who wrote this wrong wrong answer! I feel that I am a fool but, in fact, I am clever. Sometimes I think I am the cleverest girl in the class...but I made a fool's mistake.

Yesterday when she reached school, my friend—let's call her Mary—was crying and I asked her what happened? She said that she saw a dead man in front of the door of her house. She was the first one to open the door and she was the first one to see him and she began to shout and her uncle came and covered him.

"That's OK," my other friend told her, "You saw a dead man in front of your house, but I saw a dead man without a head. And another dead man who only had one foot."

I know this is scary, but it's real. And I was more scared when I heard they found fourteen dead men in Mosul. I don't know if that man that Mary saw was one of them. But it is still scary.

Yesterday at 4:30, we heard a loud boom near our house and the American tanks came around the neighborhood. One of them stopped in front of our house. We called my father and told him not to come home coz they were shooting at all the cars that tried to cross. My father used another road to come home. He could only reach the house behind our house...but he climbed the wall using a ladder and he finally reached home safely.

Something wrong

Good morning, it's eight o'clock. I know I should be in school but the bridges are closed and there is a curfew.

At about 6:45 a.m. we heard a lot of bullets and explosions. I was checking my information because I have a history examination. My sister called and said please don't go to school. We didn't know yet that the bridges were closed, but when we found out, we decided not to go and we called our friends and relatives to tell them not to go out to school or work. So I will not go to school. I will not take a history exam. Huh.

Yesterday I was unlucky on my examination. Oooof. My marks are not good like the years before. Anyway, I did my best and I understand the lesson. That's enough. Like my father said, I should not care if I have a bad mark when I understand the lesson.

I read this poem and want you to read it.

When I say... I am a Muslim
I'm not shouting
"Down with Christians and Jews."
I am whispering, "I seek peace"
And Islam is the path that I choose.
When I say...I am a Muslim,
I speak of this with pride,
And confess that sometimes I stumble
And need Allah to be my guide.
When I say...I am a Muslim,
I know that makes me strong
And in those times when I am weak

I pray to Allah for strength to carry on.
When I say...I am a Muslim,
I'm not boasting of success,
I'm acknowledging that Allah has rescued me
And I cannot ever repay the debt.
When I say...I am a Muslim,
I'm not claiming to be perfect.
My flaws are indeed visible
But Allah forgives
Because his followers are worth it.
When I say...I am a Muslim,
It does not mean I will never feel pain.
I still have my share of heartaches
Which is why I invoke Allah's name.
When I say...I am a Muslim,
I do not wish to judge.
I have no such authority.
My duty is to submit
To Allah's all-encompassing love.

I hope you liked it.

Dreams and Nightmares

WEDNESDAY, JANUARY 5
The silent life we lived

Hello people.

I know I should be studying but my mother gave me an hour to play on the Internet. I had three tests. I did well on them but now I will have fourteen more in the next ten days. I need your prayers...I should do my best; studying is the only thing I can do for Iraq these days.

The situation is so bad now. Last night when I went to bed I was thinking about the silent life that we lived before. No explosions! No bullets! How strange! Now we can sleep with loud sounds. They don't prevent us from sleeping because it has become normal. Something we hear all the time, like the sound of a bird. Last night when we heard the sound of the explosion, Aya didn't even wake up. Is she brave or what?

Hadiya in wonderland

Day after day, my laziness increases and I do not write this post. But here I am writing to you after a long time.

I took my exams and did well in most of them except for physics. What you should know is that all the bridges were closed that day and it was a big problem to get to school for those who lived on the other side of the river. Many could not come. Others used their feet and walked across the bridges. It took them one or two hours to walk to their exams!

One of the teachers came to where we were taking the exam and told us the poor old guard of our school was killed by the American soldiers today. All the girls began to cry. The big problem here is that the guard has ten children and one of them is blind and his wife has been sick for a year. So how can they live without food or money? The schoolmaster took donations from the girls and gave them to the guard's family.

I am so mad at Al-Jazeera and Al-Arabia's news because they only take the news that they agree with. The best thing that Al-Jazeera said was that it is "the wrong war in the wrong place with the wrong enemy." Blah Blah Blah.

The next day after we finished with the exams, we went to Baghdad! Yahoo! I was so excited I would be in Baghdad! Baghdad the beautiful! Baghdad, the heart of Iraq.

The road between Mosul and Baghdad was hard and difficult.

There were bombs in front of us and bombs in back of us. We were like Rambo.

We needed three hours to go to Samerah and the road from Samerah to Baghdad needs three hours more. The distance between Mosul and Samerah is about 300 kilometers and then another 100 kilometers to get to Baghdad. So after six hours of suffering, we reached Baghdad.

I saw Baghdad before but this is not the Baghdad I used to know. Something changed. I can't describe it. There is no water or electricity in Baghdad now. You feel disappointed when you open the tap and no water comes out. The water did not come out for four days.

My uncle said laughing that we should vote for Ayad Allawi because in a second we will have water and electricity. It will be a miracle!

About the election, I don't know anyone who will go and vote. We can't just go and vote. If you want my opinion, I am with the royalty. I think it's the best.

FRIDAY, JANUARY 28

Can you help me to shout?

I was thinking last night when I went to sleep: Did the American soldiers come to Iraq to give us our freedoms, which we need?

I ask myself this question and got the answer: NO! Why? I will give you a simple example.

I don't put my real name on this blog because I'm not allowed to have a free opinion in this life. I can't tell the truth until I am sure that no one knows who I am.

Plenty of things happen and I don't write about it because of you. You don't live in Iraq. You don't know what is happening here and you want to impose your opinions on me and make me believe what I say is wrong. Isn't that what you call "brainwashing"?

I want the American soldiers to get out of Iraq as soon as possible. If they settle down in Iraq they will kill us. Probably they won't kill us with their bullets but they kill our hearts more and more with their behavior.

Today, the Mosul news announced that they would tell us the election lists soon. The election will be on Sunday and they still haven't announced the lists? What happened to the world?

There will be a curfew from tomorrow until next Tuesday. Iraqi people should not walk in the street and go out and see their country, this country that they built with their hands. Can you help me to shout?

I told you before about the water in Baghdad—that there was none in the days that we were there. But I didn't tell you about the water we were drinking when it finally came out of the tap. I studied in school that water doesn't have a color, odor, or taste. From my tap, I discovered I was wrong. So was I drinking water or something else?

MONDAY JANUARY 31

A historic day come and gone

Look what I found in MSN's question of the day: "Iraqi election success: do you believe this is a turning point?" 66% voted yes, 34% no.

A historic day has come and gone.

Good morning. Yes, today is my turn on the computer. Read my post NOW because I wrote it for you.

I will talk about the election—the one you came here to read about. Yesterday was Election Day and most of the Iraqis went and voted despite the danger of this step. So that's great and I hope it will still be great after the announcement of the results. I am so afraid of the results. I try to be optimistic. Some of the people in my family went and voted and that made me feel good about myself.

About my holiday, it will end tomorrow. But we will not go back to school because of the situation. Yesterday and the days before that I was working in the kitchen with my mom. We made some sweets together. Cream puffs and sweet rolls. The sweet rolls didn't come out right but we changed their look and I think Najma and my dad loved them.

When Hadiya was a child

When I was a child, I loved to paint. The pictures were not from my imagination. I put a picture in front of my eyes and tried to draw it. The result is something different from the real picture but it works. It's beautiful...

Hey, if you like it, tell me. If you didn't like them, don't tell me. Well, I love them all. Maybe they're not so nice to you but they remind me of me in the past.

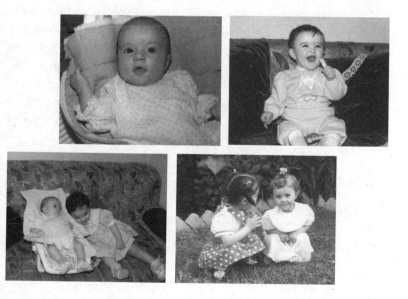

A sad girl in a small motion picture

Salam all.

School began last Saturday and I got my grades and they were somehow good.

Well, today we had to move to another school close to ours. We moved after the headmistress came to our class and ordered the teacher to leave because the rooms were full of water and the door that we called "the bridge" (because we used it as a bridge to get out of the school) was starting to sink and if we didn't go out then, we would never be able to leave. I hope we never go back to that dirty school. But in the new school, we had sixty girls in a class. Some had seventy.

After class, I was trying to find Najma. I hadn't seen her since we reached the new school together. I walked and walked back to the old school and couldn't find her or my dad who was coming to pick us up. I was in a bad state. I was carrying my heavy bag and I was tired and I wanted to cry. I went back to the new school and asked my friend Mass if she had seen Najma and just then I saw my sister and ran to her before she disappeared. I was running very slowly and imagined myself in a small motion picture. I hugged Najma—in the movie, heh. After that, everything became better. My mom and dad came to take us home and they bought kabob for lunch. And after I finished lunch, what did you expect me to do in this cold winter? I went to sleep (without having a nightmare).

FRIDAY, FEBRUARY 11
Snow

Let me present to you the Groom—ICE MAN—and the bride, Mrs. ICE. Aren't they cute? Best wishes to them to live a happy life together. Just joking.

Well, this year was the second year in a row that I saw snow. But this year, the snow dissolved after an hour and we couldn't make a snowman. I took this photo last year.

I haven't heard from Aya for two days because the telephone is not working. The only thing that I know is that she ate a potato for dinner yesterday.

SUNDAY, FEBRUARY 13

Florence

Now it's been thirty-eight days since you disappeared and I feel the omnipresence of your absence. Absence of a journalist involved in the defense of democratic values; absence of a very appreciated woman.

Now it is thirty-eight days and there is a lack in the journalist profession as if some letters in the word "liberty" were missing.

It's absolutely certain that the pen of the journalist and the image of the photograph are essential defenses facing war, facing executions, facing corruption. I still do not understand how one can kidnap or murder.

Today I read nearly 1,800 sympathy messages for you, on the websites of *Libération* and Reporters Without Borders. I read them all. Only a few come from your colleagues. Even so, certainly your kid-

---

By 2005, journalists who operated independently of the U.S. military were being regularly kidnapped in Iraq. On January 5, 2005, Florence Aubenas, a journalist with the French newspaper *Libération*, was kidnapped along with her Iraqi interpreter, Hussein Hanoun al-Saadi. The two were finally released five months later, on June 11, 2005. Here, Hadiya's letter to Florence also references many other journalists kidnapped in Iraq, and one kidnapped in Colombia.

nappers have direct access to these. Since the beginning of the invasion of Iraq, we've noticed that terrorist and Islamist fighters are masters in the art of communication over the Internet. But where? Where is the support of thousands of journalists, press correspondents, photographers, local reporters, journalism students? The more the days flow, the less I understand these absences.

So Florence, all that is too much. Much too much. Get back soon! And give meaning to the word "liberty." Then, I hope we will work together to resolve others' unwillingness to understand. No more Ingrid Betancourt, Enzo Baldoni, Abdel Hussein Khazaal, Guy-André Kieffer, Fred Nerac, Giuliana Sgrena and many others – faces on the cover of world newspapers or stuck to the front of town halls!

FRIDAY, FEBRUARY 18

Am I the one who is walking on the road or is it the road that is moving? Or are we both standing but is it the time that is running?...I don't know

Well, well.

I'm not doing well in English. I wrote "hard" when I meant "heart." I am really bad. You can say that to my face. I got nine on the English test while all the other girls in my class got ten. ALL OF THEM! Twenty-nine girls got ten and Hadiya got nine. Can you believe it?

On the same day that I got this bad mark, I had a really bad nightmare. I was killing this one girl. She was really a nice and cute girl. After school, all the girls went home and there were only eight of us left: me, Najma, the girl who I killed in my dream, and five other girls. When I looked at the girl I killed in my dream, I wanted to cry. Finally, she went home.

My father called us and said the road was closed and he couldn't come right now and asked us to wait. We were so worried about how we would get home. One of the girls had a little money left in her mobile account and her cousin told her that she had better call her parents. You know what she answered? "I only have enough in my account for one call. So if I made it now and we died, the people would not be able to use my mobile to call our parents to tell them that we had died." Strange, huh??

My father called again and said he had told my cousin to come take us home. To my surprise, my father and my cousin reached the school at the same time. One minute ago, we didn't have anyone to take us home and now there were two cars waiting for us...

I looked at my schoolbag and I saw a tear on it and I thought it must be Najma's, that I'd taken her bag and she'd taken mine. But she said she had her own schoolbag with her. "Ahhh," I shouted, "dad go back! I took someone else's schoolbag." I saw the girl we had been talking to and ran to her and gave her the bag without saying anything. I was so confused because just then there was a shelling of bullets. I left the girl with her mouth wide open like she didn't understand what I had done.

It was a really hard day but that was just the beginning. When we got home, we heard on the news how they assassinated al-Hariri, the Lebanese Muslim leader. I do not know what to say to the Lebanese people for losing their leader. I am so sorry.

SATURDAY, FEBRUARY 19
Aya's surprise

Yesterday when we finished our courses, I went out and saw my father waiting for me with Aya. SURPRISE! All my friends came to see Aya. There were thirteen girls in all. So Aya was having a good time like a princess. And she is a princess to me.

On the way home, the traffic policeman told us not to go down our street because it was closed so we left the car and walked. My mother ran to us and carried Aya inside as quickly as she could because the bullets are coming very close to our house.

The point of this post is that we are suffering from closed roads. We are suffering from our bad schools. These hard days are unforgettable but we need to forget this bad part of our lives. We need to erase it or change it. But we can't run from the truth.

I will go now to play with Aya and pray to do well in my English examination tomorrow. Bye now and see you soon. Inshallah.

TUESDAY, FEBRUARY 22

Is this school or what?

Good morning. Would you like to go to my school? Come with me. Yallah (Let's go)!!!

Stand on this brick to reach my school. If you are afraid, there is another way. Use this but be careful not to fall in the pond. Oh, you reached the swamp. Sorry—IT'S MY SCHOOL.

This view you can see from the window of my classroom.

Can you believe that I am going to this school every day? And I breathe this polluted air with my friends? Is this school or what??

God knows what microbe I just breathed in. Surely I am sick now and I don't know it. Help us!! I don't know how but we need your help. So hellllllllllllllllllllllp us if you can.

Note—my school's name is al-Mutamiezat school.

Yours,

The suffering girl (Hadiya)

FROM JEFF:

Are you a good swimmer?
...Okay, let's do it! I'm serious. Who is in charge of coordinating projects from the American side in Mosul? Who is the person in charge in the Ministry of Education in Mosul who fixes these problems? Who does the principal of the school talk to about problems?
Step-by-step will solve the problems. Patience and step-by-step.

FROM HADIYA:

Well, the principal says that she called al-Iraqia, Mosul's TV station, and told them about our school's problem. Two days later, the governor of Mosul called her. He was mad at her for doing that, and didn't give us any help.

The same thing happened when the director of al-Salam's hospital told the TV station how the Americans occupied the hospital: the governor of Mosul was very mad at the director and kept telling him that there were no Americans in the hospital (but, there were, and everyone knows it).

[Anyway, they said that our school was on TV a few days ago, but this didn't help.]

Sick from school

Hello all.

Guess what? My school's microbes are too active!!!

Yes yes, I am sick now. I don't like to be sick. Ever.

I couldn't play with Aya or sit near her. She looked at me and talked to me and said, "waaawaaahhh waaawaaahhh." I don't know what that means in baby language but she was waiting for me to play with her I guess.

"Aaaaaaaaaaahhh." Hadiya's language is not so different from the baby's language.

Am I silly today?

Well, I am sick.

Bye-bye.

Sisters and friends

I was thinking about my friends. I consider them my sisters— Mass, Mary, and Hanan. They all let you feel like you're their sisters.

Let's talk about Hanan. Hanan is Christian and she is one of my BEST BEST friends. I told her today that I feel she is like me and she said that she felt that way too. The point is that our religion is not in conflict with our friendship. We are all from Adam.

Did I talk to you about how Najma treats Aya? I don't think so. Najma usually brings something that Aya likes to eat and dangles it in front of her eyes. But when Aya reaches her hands to take it, her aunt takes it away. Well, that is Najma. What can a little sister (me) do about that?

Me and Najma are so different in everything. If you ask me who is the strong one and who is the wronged one, I will tell you. Until

2001, I was the strong one and I could control Najma but she learned to run away from me. So I lost my control and now I am the wronged girl.

Don't think that Najma is a good girl, because she isn't. She is perfect and that makes her the bad girl in my eyes. Yes, I am jealous of her. Yes, I am. Don't laugh. It's killing me to say this. So the only way to stop talking is to say bye-bye.

THURSDAY, MARCH 24
Get me out of here

Thank you all for supporting me. Most of you must be wondering why I haven't posted for a long time. That is because I am busy with exams, which will not end until next month...

They built a new school for us in front of our old school. They told us we will move into it next week. I hope they told us the truth.

I will tell you another problem that I have. I have discovered that 95 percent of the girls in my class cheat on the examinations. I don't know what's happening with the people. Is it only me that feels that there are more bad people than good ones?

Alima was one of my best friends until this year when she began walking with a bad girl who does not respect the teachers and cheats and does many things I don't like. When I don't like someone, I can't change my mind about her. So this year I didn't only lose my good marks but I lost my friend Alima and I lost my confidence in people and in myself.

I don't know why I am feeling this way. I need something to do and make me feel better about myself. Let's see, what do you think would help me? I want to discover something or do something that lets me win the Nobel Prize. I want to learn how to make stuff. I want to learn English good so when I write something you can understand me and not laugh.

I want to say to all the mothers who are reading my post right now to be proud of yourselves. You are great women! And I want to tell everyone to take care of their parents and look after them. When you treat your parents well, your children will treat you as well as you treat your parents.

That reminds me of this story. There was an ill man who was having trouble walking on his feet. His son saw that his father was tired so he carried him on his back. The father began to cry and the son asked him why he was crying. His father replied, "I remember myself twenty-five years ago when I carried my father on my back in this place."

Give more. Get more.

WEDNESDAY, MARCH 30

Good, better, and best news

Do you want to hear good tidings? My mother asked us to take care of Aya when she and my big sister went shopping. Najma wanted the first two hours but she changed her mind after I told her she might have to change Aya's diaper and feed her milk. That's work. So I got the first two hours.

Aya was quiet and nice... I searched on the Internet and found songs for children. She was amused to listen to them.

Last night, our neighbor came to our house with her son who is four or five years old. He was sick so my father had to inject [some medicine into] him. The boy cried and Aya began to laugh—did she understand what was going on and thought it was funny? I don't know.

Anyway, my sister asked him to stop crying and said the American soldiers would laugh at him. He said, "Let them laugh at me. Let them kill me. Let them cut my head off. I don't mind. Let them do what they want." I joined Aya and began to laugh too.

When we were children, my father refused to give us injections when we were sick. My cousins avoided my father when he went to their house because he always gave them injections and they were afraid of him. My father refused to inject any one of us so he wouldn't make us hate him. He didn't know that we would still love him whatever he did.

Yesterday, one of my friends from primary school who I hadn't seen for nine years called me. It was really a surprise to me that she had saved my number and still remembered me after all these years. I told her that I was an aunt now and she said she had a niece too.

Last good news that I have to tell you is that today we went and saw our new school and it looked like they will finish it in the next few days. Yahooooo!

Falsely accused

Yesterday was a really bad day. When the teacher entered the class, I asked her a small question and she said she would not answer me because during the last examination she had asked me and the other girls if we had a mobile phone "and you said NO and I knew that you had one but you wouldn't let me take it."

I said I don't have a mobile phone.

"I know you have one. I was not sure then but now I am."

I asked her to check my bag. But she said, "Maybe you didn't bring it with you today, but the day of the exam you did." After a long speech, I discovered that I am a liar and that I don't listen to the teacher's orders.

I swear I don't have a mobile phone and I didn't bring one with me to school but what could I do? I told her the truth but she didn't believe me.

After that I began to cry and my friends (well, not only my friends but all the girls in the class) came to me and said they know that I didn't have one and told me not to listen to the teacher. I am still feeling bad.

Today, I woke up at 6 a.m. and prayed and I began writing and working on my homework until the electricity went off. In the afternoon, we went with my uncle to the north and had a great time there but when we came home there was a surprise waiting for us.

When we reached the traffic light, there was a burned car with parts of it everywhere. The windows of the bakery were all broken out and the police would not let us go to our street because the Americans were coming. The policeman told my father to go back but my father told him that our house is on that road. That is your responsibility the policeman said so we went home and were safe but it was a really bad surprise.

MONDAY, APRIL 25

I will not wait anymore

Guess what happened to your friend Hadiya?
She got A's in all her subjects.
Oh yeah! I did it!

I know I haven't posted in a long time and you missed me so much. So did I. I'll talk about my new school. It's a good school. We have a large yard and I lose my friends in it all the time. I spend all my time looking for them. Najma always asks me why I'm not walking with my friends.

But the real problem is that our classroom and many other classes have windows facing the street. So when the bullets begin to rain, we don't know what to do...

Last week was really bad. We couldn't reach home. We often had to leave the car somewhere else and walk home on foot. Now I know why I have lost four kilos (nine pounds)...

The situation is so bad. It really is getting worse all the time. But we didn't care about our lives and went on a picnic with the family.

My English teacher told us to write something about our future and what we want to be. I gave her my homework and she read it and laughed but she won't make any comment until tomorrow.

Oh, I remember that I won't go to school tomorrow. All the girls who got A's don't have to go.

I took some sweets with me to school to give them to the teachers. When I entered the teachers' room, my legs began to tremble. The first teacher looked at me and asked if Baysan was my aunt. I said yes and she told me that she saw me when I was a little girl in her house. Thank God she didn't begin to tell me what a cute little girl I was.

The next teacher said what a polite girl I am. Another teacher asked why I would give them sweets? Of course it was because of my success. The next teacher stood up and told everyone I was Najma's sister. And the next teacher. And the next. AAAAAAAAAAH! They make me crazy!

Yesterday, the computer teacher came to my class and told the English teacher that she wanted me. The English teacher said, "Najma's sister, come here!" Then the computer teacher told the English teacher, "She doesn't like to be called Najma's sister," and the English teacher said, "I know." How cute these teachers are.

I want to learn how to speak French well this vacation but I don't know how. I want to learn many things but I do not know how to learn them and if there is enough time to learn them all.

Two days ago was Najma's birthday but I couldn't go out of the house to buy her a gift so I asked her to choose three kinds of sweets to make for her. I made cream puffs and cream caramel and another one but I don't know its name in Arabic so I can't tell you it in English.

Baghdad

One week without writing a post makes for a lot of news. What can we do? Iraqi life is really active.

As you know I finished my school last week so I could go with my mother and Najma to visit my grandparents in Baghdad.

The road leading to Baghdad was not really good. To be more clear, there were two booby traps—one of them had not exploded yet. So we changed our route. And the other road was all smashed up.

Anyway, we reached Baghdad and what happened last time we went there happened again. I want to visit Baghdad all the time BUT when I get there, I want to get out.

We visit Baghdad every six months so between the two last visits, there were big changes. It has gotten worse. I used to see Baghdad like a paradise. That was in Saddam's time.

This visit to Baghdad was the first since my uncle Ahmad left. You know how much parents miss their sons? So imagine how sad my grandmother and grandfather were when he left.

Our visit helped to return the smile to their faces. My cousin moved into my grandparents' home so there was a person who could play with us. He taught me, Najma, and Raghda how to play badminton. We were all bad at it and my mother and my grandparents didn't stop laughing at us but we became better. I also played chess and won when I played Raghda and her brother but I couldn't beat my cousin.

One day when Najma, Raghda, her brother, my cousin, and I were sitting with my grandfather, I asked him which group did he prefer? Najma, Raghda, and me or the boys' group? He said he preferred the girls.

And when we asked my grandmother which group she liked best, she said "I love you all." You don't know my grandmother. She has a big heart that has space for all the world.

We stayed in Baghdad for five days before coming back to Mosul. When we got home, my mom asked me to cook something that is easy for me. I couldn't think of anything. Do you know that I incinerated the dessert I made yesterday? But I am not a bad woman all the time. I can clean the kitchen and I made it SO clean. Tomorrow, I will go with my father to pick out a gift for myself.

See you soon.

I am an Iraqi girl!

Yeahooooo! Now I can say that I am an Iraqi girl. I got my Iraqi citizenship three days ago. [In Iraq, you apply for citizenship when you may need it, much like applying for a passport in the U.S.]

I also went with my father and bought my present. He bought me a CD/DVD/Cassette MP3 player. Najma helped me to find some songs from the Internet and we copied them to a CD. I found many Omkalthoom songs, Fayrouze's songs, Abdul Aleem's songs.

I am busy these days with Aya and homework. Najma has begun her studies so she can't spend time with us like before. Yesterday, I was alone in the house and I heard the sound of bullets so I rushed to the window to see if the road was closed. Najma came after some minutes and she looked pale. She told me the bullets had come too close and they had seen a man pointing a gun at a policeman. Najma's friend began to cry when the bullets broke up near them.

Well, every family in Iraq spends time like this every day. This is why we should pay tribute to America because it gives us the freedom that we want. Note: Freedom means doing what you want even if it's wrong and you shouldn't do it. You are free to kill what you want. Steal anybody you want and anything you like.

Only, I studied history and discovered that freedom should be something useful.

Sounds in the night and sights in the day

Salam all,

I am really tired now. I couldn't sleep well last night because there were sounds of helicopters all the night – as usual, so I don't know why I could sleep the days before but not yesterday.

My sister said policemen were killed near the hospital where she works and she saw a lot of patients who had been attacked and killed by bullets and bombs. Therefore, people, I don't want to be a doctor. I am not sure that I can see someone hurting. When I see these images on TV, I can't sleep well. So how could I see them in front of my eyes?

Yesterday, we found two newspapers in front of our house. It seems the American soldiers put them there. IT IS FREE! This means we won't have to spend 250 dinars to buy a newspaper. Heh!

P.S. It seems like I like myself b'coz I used "I" more than twenty times in this blog. OK, I will shut up.

WEDNESDAY, MAY 18

The nightmare

Aya and Najma and I were alone in the house. Aya and I were asleep when Najma woke us up and said that a cousin who works in a shop near our house called and said there is a mine in front of our street so we should go to the safe room and open all the windows. We did what he said. At the time, there was nothing strange—just the sound of helicopters.

After some minutes, the nightmare began. We heard the sound of bombs exploding and shelling. We didn't know what was happening. I ran and carried Aya and we sat on the bed far from the window. Me and Najma sang to Aya so she wouldn't be scared. Then a big bomb went off and smashed the window and we hugged each other. Everybody began to call us to ask what was happening. I didn't know exactly. It seemed like the nightmare lasted two months, not two hours. After some time, the road was opened and first my mother and then my father came home. As Najma said and all the neighbors agreed, never in the war have we had such a horrible day.

What happened made me feel sure that the American army is an occupation force not anything else.

Stay in peace.

SUNDAY, MAY 22

I am what I am, Mr. Anonymous

You hurt me and you hurt me a lot. Therefore I deleted your comments. You shouldn't write something like that to me. You don't know what I am. WHO I AM.

I don't care about your choice to not be a Muslim. But I do care about my destiny. I haven't had a good and happy life, and that was not my option. But I do have the option to choose how my destiny will be, so I choose to be happy, I choose to be a Muslim from the second I was born to my last breath.

Brilliant! What is this stupid question: "From what planet are you coming from?" Is there any option for me to live somewhere else than the Earth? I was created to live in Iraq but that also was not my choice. I do love Iraq. But I can't stand more of this.

Another anonymous said, "You certainly don't deserve this life." I want to ask you something—is this really a life?

Last night, I cried all through the night like I have never cried before. I am really tired of living BUT IT'S MY FATE.

TUESDAY, MAY 24
Words

Today we had a visitor. My sister's friend came to congratulate her for her new baby. What irony! Aya is now nine months old. But her friend couldn't come until today because they were waiting for the situation to get better, but it only got worse.

My English is bad and some people understand my post in a wrong way. Remember when I remarked about American freedom in Iraq and said "Freedom is doing what you want even if it's wrong. You are free to kill anything you want. Steal anybody or anything you like?" Some understood that this is what I believe but what I meant was I reject it. I admit that I don't have a good way to explain my view of life and my bad English helps the people who want to make me weaker and sadder than I am. I mean to say something and instead say something else.

For example, I don't know if I should say my OLD sister or my BIG sister or my LARGE sister. It's all the same to me. I can say that I am only fifteen years old—but this will change in one week when I am sixteen and I won't be able to use that argument anymore.

THURSDAY, MAY 26
Holiday days

I am OK and I am getting better because of the nice people who stand with me. For the first time in a long time, I opened my e-mail and there were seven new messages.

You know, I am on holiday now. Other students who did not receive all A's are still taking their examinations. I am spending this holiday on the Internet. One day for me and one day for Najma. On Najma's turn on the computer, Aya usually comes to our house so I don't feel the time pass slowly.

First, I go to the kitchen and boil her an egg. Then the fun begins. We play a game that is called in Arabic بح دي. I hide behind something and after a few seconds I appear. Maybe you think it's silly but to Aya it's not. And it's really a popular game for children in Mosul. She also likes to swing on the swing until she gets tired.

I also spend time watching television. I watch *Gilmore Girls*, *Popular*, *Friends*, *According to Jim*, *Scrubs*, *Frasier*, and *Eight Simple Rules*. I like all of them.

Our telephone hasn't worked for four weeks and more. So if you called me and nobody answered, this is the reason. (Just kidding.) Half the year the telephone works, the other half it doesn't. And the electricity is worse. We had a neighborhood generator and sometimes we found ourselves in the dark and the heat. Between 12 in the morning and 12 at night, 90 percent of the time we have no electricity. God knows what will happen in the next month. We are in May and it is already hot so what will happen in June and July? Note: July is the month of the hottest weather in Iraq...

SATURDAY, MAY 28

Days come, days go

Yesterday we left our house for the first time this week. We went to visit my uncle, who we had not seen for a month. After that we went to buy dinner. We went to three shops and all of them were closed. At the end, we bought بعجين لحم (Lahmacun)—it's something like pizza but it's not pizza. This is the first time we went out. CAN YOU BELIEVE THAT? There were not many cars in the street.

Talking about electricity in my last post, I forgot to say that we didn't have electricity in Saddam's time too. Baghdad was the only place to have electricity twenty-four hours but that changed after the war began. All the cities became equal now because all of them don't have electricity most of the day.

When I was a little girl, I once asked my mother if there is any country where there is electricity all day? I couldn't imagine that! How could they have electricity all the time when we only had four to seven hours of it? And many days, we didn't have any electricity at all. Sometimes when I remember things like that from when I was a kid, I feel sorry for myself.

Today I saw a TV program called "Yallah Shabab." They were in the U.S. at one of the big universities in California. They asked the people there about the Iraq War and what they thought about Islam and did they want to learn Arabic? One of the girls answered really nicely. She said, "I don't like sending our sons to fight your sons and daughters." The point is this war is between our governments and not the peoples so we shouldn't hate each other. In the end, we are all from Adam. So I want to say that I don't hate U.S. people.

David my friend posts nice pictures that he took when he went to the zoo. I wrote him a letter and said I had never gone to a zoo. He replied that he never went to a zoo until he was twenty-five so I had ten years to catch up. BUT you don't see, my friend—Iraq has no zoos. Yes, we have some small places where they'll post a cartoon and write the word "Zoo." People who visit there say there are only dogs, cats, a horse, a donkey, a camel, and a bear there—animals that we can see on our way to school. What a strange country I live in!!!

Yesterday, we bought powdered milk. It cost 1,350 dinar while before the war it was only 350. Maybe the salaries have increased, but now all the stuff costs more than before. I know 1,350 dinar is cheap but 350 is cheaper.

Before the war, if anyone wanted ice cream and it was 12 o'clock at night, we would get in the car and go buy the ice cream. Every Friday, we went out and had dinner outside. And every Thursday, we would visit all my aunts and uncles—we called this day "the meeting day." The wedding parties would start at night while now there are only two options: not do the wedding party or have it between four and seven in the afternoon.

Sometimes, I just want to be a kid again and live in the days before the war began but it's just a dream. I hope I will live to spend times nicer and more beautiful than these days.

Yours, Hadiya

MONDAY, MAY 30

Hadiya the servant

Hi and welcome.

Today I washed the dishes and cleaned the grounds and made the salad and prepared the food and the fruit. Mom didn't ask me to wash the dishes but there was no electricity and I didn't have anything else to do.

I began reading a book. The name is *Hayati (My Life)* by Ahmad Amin, who rose to a leading role in Egypt's cultural life and is well known for tracing the story of Islam from what he called its "Dawn" to "High Noon." This is what the *Middle East Journal*, Vol. 9, Number 11, London 1955, wrote about him: "The book *Hayati* is the life of the distinguished Cairo scholar and educator and is impressive in its simplicity and sincerity."

I began reading this book two days ago and it looks like I will finish it today. I found something useful in reading it.

Aya was here today. She was like a princess and I was an evil servant who made her take a nap. After she was sleeping for a long time, me and Najma decided to wake her to play with her. She was so quiet and with good manners too. Oh Aya, I never loved a baby as much as I love her.

I need to nap now.

TUESDAY, MAY 31

YAHOOOOO!!
Don't worry, I am happy NOW.

This week was happy. Your prayers were useful to me. Well, I want to tell you something but please don't laugh at me. I ate a cherry for the first time in my life! There were no cherries in Iraq and now it looks like they have begun to import them from outside. This is one of the positive things that happened after the war. Now we can choose from Iraqi oranges, Syrian oranges, Turkish oranges, and Egyptian oranges. Of course we do not choose the Iraqi oranges because they are too small compared to the others.

We are in summer and the summer fruit begins to appear. I like eating fruit—especially watermelon for lunch. "Yummy."

Yesterday I took my book and read until 1 a.m. Then I tried to sleep but I couldn't. The electricity was turned off and I thought this was the reason. But then the generator came on and I thought oh finally I will sleep but I couldn't. After a long time, I looked at the clock and it said 3:15. WOW! I should be dreaming now. Then I remembered that I drank some Nescafe instant coffee and that was certainly the reason I didn't sleep.

Guess what happened? Our telephone got fixed this afternoon. I called my friend Mary and asked her to visit me someday, but she told her father and he refused because of the bad explosions that happen in our neighborhood. He doesn't think our house is a safe place for his daughter to visit. This feels weird to me because this is the same neighborhood that I've lived in since I was born.

I am laughing right now. Somebody called and I picked up the phone. "Alo," I said.

"Alo, who are you?"

"Who are you?

"Well, I don't know what to say to you. Do you have any brothers?"

"NO! What do you want?"

"Well, I don't know what to say...My daughter told me that someone called who had this number...so I called back, but it seems you didn't call us and you are not a boy."

It was strange. I understood him. Some boys call girls just to annoy them. Isn't that the most stupid manners?

I noticed that my mother bought my birthday gift today. When I entered her room she tried to push me out. Well, she won. I love surprises so I don't want to know what it is. So I will wait...

FRIDAY, JUNE 3

I am sixteen

Thank you for your sweet comments and e-mails. I am certainly happy because I have friends like you and this is the greatest gift I have received. I will celebrate tomorrow with my family and Aya because my mother is sick today. I hope she will be fine tomorrow so we can make a cake together. I wanted to share this picture with you

when I was about sixteen months old. Well, now I am sixteen years. SIXTEEN! He he he.

I got my present. It's a nice green sports t-shirt. I like it.

Your sixteen-age friend.

Stuck

Hi all,

Today for the third time this week I went out "not normal."

Some days before when I didn't leave home for a long time, and I looked outside and saw the sky, I don't know what happened to me. It was like it was the first time I saw it, and I just wanted to cry.

I have a problem here: every movement in the house, every thing that happens I write in my mind as a post in the blog. And that is bothering me a little. Well, what else do I have to say????

Today my father and I went together to pick up Najma from her friend's house and while we were in the road we didn't speak at all. NOBODY talked till I said: "Dad, I was at home, so I don't have anything to say, but surely you do?" Then my dad said about ten words and stopped. And while we were in the road there were many helicopters above us. And after that there were about six tanks in the road. So we stopped the car and waited with the other people who were there. And after some minutes they moved and so did we.

Yes, I am blaming again

The bad electricity service that we have here in Iraq doesn't give us more than four hours in a day. On lucky days, we get seven.

That pushed my dad to buy us a light that works on batteries so we can do our homework when the electricity goes off. Everyone in the family has his own flashlight. Mine is blue. My sister's is red. It is the most useful thing to spend your money on.

But that is not enough for a country that doesn't have electricity most of the time.

Here is another picture of our suffering. Najma talked about it in her blog. This is the electricity traffic light. It's in the entrance of our home. The green light means "the electricity is on." The yellow light means "the neighborhood's generator is on." The blue light means "the neighbor's generator is on." Each family has to know the kind of electricity they are using.

Well, we have a traffic light.

Did you hear this joke?

A man was taking a walk in Central Park in New York. Suddenly he sees a little girl being attacked by a pit bull. He runs over and starts fighting with the dog, and succeeds in killing the dog and saving the girl's life.

A policeman who was watching the scene walks over and says: "You are a hero, tomorrow you can read it in all the newspapers: *Brave New Yorker saves the life of little girl!*"

The man says: "But I am not a New Yorker!"

"Oh, then it will say in newspapers in the morning: *Brave American saves life of little girl!*"

"But I am not an American!" answers the man.

"Oh, what are you then?" the policeman asks.

The man says, "I am a Pakistani."

The next day the newspaper says: *Islamic extremist kills innocent American dog.*

Water!

Clear water, dirty water. It doesn't trouble us. We drink both.

My uncle's house water has a small fish in it. We get used to the taste and the color but fish? It is another problem.

We heard about many people being poisoned by water so my father bought us a new water cooler.

My biology teacher told us not to drink the water because it's dirty. But some people said that we have an immunity because we have drunk dirty water for years. But certainly it was not as bad as it is now.

We heard some news that people were killed and their bodies thrown in the river. So maybe the water that we drink...you know. I can't say it.

WEDNESDAY, JUNE 15
I am blind, I can't see the truth

One month ago, I wrote about this problem I have. I have nightmares every night. I really hate what has happened to me. I've discovered that the real life I live is a nightmare. The truth became clear and its features began to appear... I was running from the truth. I can't agree with what has happened here but I also can't confess that I lived a better life and spent beautiful times in Saddam's time.

In fact, I hated Saddam SO MUCH. But now I don't hate him. I don't like that. I don't feel anything toward him. He doesn't mean anything to me.

What was I thinking? Get what I want? Have the happy life that I dream of? See a peaceful world?

Believe or not believe. A few days ago, my sisters and my mom were watching TV. My sister, who is a doctor, turned to the al-Iraqia channel. What was there?

"Why did you cut off the head of a doctor who gave you medicine?"

In the moment we saw this we began to laugh. Bad news that you don't expect always makes you laugh.

Did they wait for the people who killed the doctors to answer? Why? What a stupid question: did the people who cut off the doctor's head recognize what they did?

I still can't believe what my eyes saw.

What should I feel toward the people who killed the doctor? Toward the soldiers who kill my relatives and my people every day? Toward Saddam who broke my heart?

What should I say? What should I feel? What should I do?

I don't know. I am blind in the dark.

As the war continued, doctors were often victimized by violence, both by insurgents (as in the incident Hadiya describes here) and by the U.S. military (as in the November 2004 invasion of Fallujah). The Red Cross has estimated that more than 2,200 doctors and nurses were killed in the first five years of the war.

FRIDAY, JUNE 17

What happened to my mind?

What happened to my mind? That was the first question that came to my mind. And my mind is still asking, what's happening to me?

Yesterday, I spent five minutes looking at the toothbrushes and wondering, Which one is mine? After that, I took my mother's toothbrush and started brushing my teeth with it. At the time, I felt that it was not mine.

My mind asks itself this day the same question: What happened to me? When Najma, my sister, went to wash the dishes she saw the pizza that I had put under the water so she came to me and seemed so angry. Why had I put the pizza there? Did I do that? Was I the one who put the pizza under the water? STRANGE.

I ask myself if I am really sixteen. Well, I looked in the mirror and saw a face that has pimples on it. So, yes, I am really sixteen.

Stop talking about my mind. My mind's work is to think and I am writing what I think so my mind always thinks what I write.

Yesterday, I went with a friend to see my friend "Mary." From the minute I walked through the door until I left, she wouldn't stop forcing me to eat. In the beginning, she gave me a lecture about how I seemed thin and how much that doesn't help my health. After that, she served me ice cream and a half hour later, a cake and cola, and then a banana and an apple and a watermelon and candy and cookies. Oh, I ate so much.

When I came home, I ate my lunch. I did not stop eating all night. Well, I haven't stopped eating for the last few days. Maybe it is because I don't feel comfortable.

We heard that American soldiers imprisoned six Iraqi women. And I heard from my sister who works at the hospital that the American soldiers took a three-year-old boy there after they shot him. Not good news to hear. If I do not talk about the bad times that are happening in Iraq, I will not find anything to talk about. At that time, I should probably shut up, close the blog, and begin counting the days.

TUESDAY, JUNE 21

STILL ALIVE!

Be optimistic. You are normal. I told you before that I think my mind has stopped working. Well, I received many e-mails from senders who told me the same thing is happening to them. "I go into a room for something and when I reach the room, I don't know why I am there."

I haven't written for a long time. Many things have happened that don't help me to be happy. Not at all. I am not in a good mind to write about it. All I can say is that today is better than yesterday.

We were so near to being killed this week. Especially my parents. The people around me are being killed and kidnapped.

Oh Allah, help us!

It's an Iraqi's life. It is my life.

Salam all. How are you people?

One of the people who works in the same building as my father called an hour ago and told my dad not to come to the clinic. There is a confrontation in the area around the clinic. But my father will take his turn anyway. No problem. He is my great dad.

The day before yesterday I was so sad so I decided to go to my room and draw something. I drew what I think was a wonderful image. Even Najma—NAJMA—who has never admitted until today that the pictures I draw are nice told me that it is beautiful. "Whew!"

Hot news. My sister just came from the hospital and said there were a lot of patients with bullet injuries today. They were shot while they were inside their houses. Yes! Inside their houses!

I told you that last week was full of danger. And I don't like to talk about that. You can read about it in my father's blog "Bad Days."

I don't like to talk about it. When I write about the bad things that happen to the Iraqi people or the bad situation, I am in a worse state than when I began.

We have big problems in Mosul this week. Fuel is not available and on the black market it costs twenty-five times more than it did before. We can't buy from a fuel station because it is too crowded. There is no hope to reach your turn even after ten hours of waiting. Half the people never get their fuel even if they wait there that long. This is Mosul's problem these days.

Baghdad has another problem. The people there don't have water. Not even polluted water. And we are in summer and this is Baghdad. So ask Allah to help them.

SUNDAY, JUNE 19

Bad days

These days are really bad, here in Mosul. There are many incidents of kidnapping, killing and hijacking.

A couple of days ago, a neighbor's son, thirty years old, married and with four children, was kidnapped from his shop in the most crowded street in Mosul. Today before noon they found his body with two bullets in his head.

Yesterday, just in front of my clinic, a car was hijacked in the middle of the day. A few hours later, the bodies of two dead guys were found 100 meters from my clinic.

This morning at 6:30 we heard about fifty explosions; later we knew they were a mortar bomb against an American base. One mortar bomb fell on the house of my close friend's brother; thank God nobody was hurt in the house.

The most striking thing is the carjacking: it is aimed at a certain car maker (BMW). The stolen cars leave the city toward the north. According to a police officer, more than seventy cars are hijacked a day. In one incident, the thieves knocked on the door of the house, and when they open the door they threatened them with gun, either to die or let the thieves take the car. From their accent, they were probably Kurds from Sulaimaniya.

There is a big shortage of gasoline these days. The line of cars at the gasoline stations may reach several kilometers. The price of gasoline at the black market is ten times its original price.

The electricity is very bad: it comes twice a day, max. Two hours each time. The neighborhood generator has stopped working because there is no diesel fuel.

The water supply for domestic use is unsterilized, it is highly contaminated, and unsuitable for human use.

Even the air is polluted from the smoke of the old cars, the diesel machine of the generators, etc.

This is our condition two years after the liberation/ occupation.

FRIDAY, JULY 1

OH GOD.

I have written many posts but I don't have the courage to publish them. I haven't gone out of the house in nine days so I have no new news.

"Day after day, the situation is getting better." That's what a high-ranking military man said. But the reality shows the opposite.

Let me remember what Najma said to me the other day: "It is better to remain silent and be thought a fool then to speak out and remove all doubt."

If it is getting better, then why don't we have water and oil while we live in a country of oil and we have two great rivers, the Tigris and the Euphrates?

We are in the third year of the war. Three years and the war does not end. So when you want to help the Iraqi people, don't send your cousins and sons to Iraq to fight because they fight us not for us.

Did you forget the WMDs?

Did you forget what happened in Abu Ghraib?

Did you forget what humanity means?

Did you forget what humans need?
Don't bother. I also forgot something.
I forgot what peace looks like.
What the street looks like.
What the sky in the night looks like.
What my relatives look like.

Sometimes I just think that if you could see what my eyes see, if you could hear what my ears hear, you would be able to understand what I mean.

Some words from the world.

Did you read what Khalid (my fellow Iraqi blogger) wrote in his blog? "I am pro God. I am pro life. I am pro humanity. I am pro truth. And when the American government chooses to be against all that, then damn it! I am anti-American government."

And at the end, I want to share with you this joke.

Are you pessimistic?

Do you feel sad, poor, and disturbed?

Congratulations! You are 100 percent Iraqi!

Another joke:

Who is an Iraqi?

An Iraqi is a human who lives in the world, is hated by the countries in the world, wronged by the media in the world, disturbed in his thoughts about the world, exploited by the governments of the world, and sad in his life in the world.

Well, this doesn't look like a joke in English, so I will write it in Arabic.

تعريف العراقي: كائن حي مكروه دوليا. مظلوم أعلاميا. مشتت ذهنيا. مثقف ماديا. مضطهد حكوميا. تعيس عمليا. منكوب يوميا

FROM ANONYMOUS:

This makes no sense. I will be happy when the American soldiers leave so Iraq can get back to whatever it thinks it was before. It was so peaceful then, wasn't it? — war with Iran, war with Kuwait, killing of the Kurds, killing in the south, such a peaceful place. I know you are not responsible, but I just don't understand WHO you support in all of this mess. If you don't like the Americans, you don't like the new government, you didn't like Saddam—please explain, if you can, who it is you do like.

FROM RACHEL IN LONDON:

This would be the war with Iran in which the USA backed Saddam Hussein with money and arms; the killing of the Kurds was with helicopters supplied by the USA for "dual purpose" (i.e., crop-spraying and gassing villagers, as the US did not bother to get any assurances from Saddam); the killing in the south was of the marsh Arabs who, emboldened by promises of help and support from the first President Bush, rose up against Saddam and then—when the promised help never arrived— were massacred and the marshes drained.

I didn't support Saddam. I've told you this again and again.

About your question, what do I like?

I like peace. I didn't live in peace before and I don't know what it looks like, but I've heard about it. And I like what people say: "World peace." Some words stay in your heart forever.

So I support the people who want peace for us, whoever they are.

TUESDAY, JULY 5

Family

Guess what? We finally went out of the house. We had a good time at my uncle's and all the family was there. All my uncles and their children and their grandchildren. This is normal in Iraq.

The people where you live don't meet their relatives as much as we do. It is normal to you that your sons move to another house before they are married. But to us, the sons live with their parents until marriage and after the marriage, some move to another house and some stay with their parents. The sons and daughters that move visit their parents at least once a week.

My mother's holiday began yesterday so I will be in contact with you more than before because Mama will take care of Aya now.

Aya controls us. She is so smart and so cute and so active too. I fought with her yesterday (but I was right) and she got angry and wouldn't look in my face until I entreated her to forgive me and then I hugged her and played with her and the princess began to smile.

SATURDAY, JULY 9

Good?

Good morning. Good evening. Good night.

I like to hear these phases because they have the word "good" in them and because my life doesn't have much good in it otherwise.

Aya fell on the ground while she was trying to climb a table and the table fell on her face and her nose began to bleed. It was the middle of the night and her mother called. She was obviously distressed and her voice sounded like she was crying. Well, I began to cry when I heard that. My sister was worried that Aya would need stitches in her nose. But thanks to Allah she didn't need them and she is fine now except that she has a red nose like a clown. The only thing she needs is to put on a red dress and she will look elegant.

Yesterday, my father's friend invited us to lunch but Najma and I didn't want to go over there. So we were alone at lunchtime. As usual, I cooked the lunch and Najma ate it. My sister—my NICE sister, my helpful sister (Najma) discovered that she hadn't done any house work lately so she went and washed the dishes of her own free will. Didn't I tell you that she likes to help other people?

Let's talk about my nice sister. I don't know what's happening to her these last few days. Before we went to sleep last night, she told me she would jump out of the window. I told her that I would jump with her. So she changed her mind. I think she doesn't like company.

Don't worry. We are Muslims. Muslim people do not commit suicide. It is not acceptable in our religion.

I think I am not doing well. I couldn't be fun.

Something happened. Knock on the table! (It is a custom in Mosul to knock on the table so no one will envy you.) I had a good dream last night. STRANGE! Did any of you have a nightmare last night? Maybe our dreams were exchanged.

OK, have a good weekend.

I don't know what to say.

In July 2005, Khalid Jarrar—another Iraqi blogger whose posts Hadiya sometimes refers to—was arrested at his Baghdad university for "reading terrorist websites." The websites in question were those of the Iraqi bloggers Raed Jarrar, Khalid's brother (raedinthemiddle.blogspot.com), and Riverbend (riverbendblog.blogspot.com). After Khalid's arrest, people around the world protested to the Iraqi government until he was released. Hadiya's sister Najma helped to create an internet petition for his release. Khalid's account of his arrest and release is online at http://secretsinbaghdad.blogspot.com/2005_07_01_archive.html.

I know I haven't posted for a long time. I wrote a post and was going to put it in my blog but the next day I visited Raed's blog, which I don't visit much. I read about what happened to Khalid and sat here all day sad and bored. That was all I needed to complete my perfect day.

My older sister advised me to stop blogging. What happened to Khalid is not a game. We should do something for him. He is the blogger known as "An Iraqi Blogger." NOW he is in jail.

Why is he there?

What is he doing there?

How is he?

I don't know.

To go back to our subject, stop blogging or not? I was thinking about this so I wrote a post talking about this freedom we have to blog. We don't need it. It is the same freedom that made Khalid write what he was thinking and the same freedom that put him in jail for writing that. So I don't need this freedom. Take it!

Pooh.

Raghda, my cousin came from Baghdad yesterday and she will leave tomorrow. We have a good time together. I will talk about that in my next post. If I continue my blog.

Pray for all of us. Heh heh heh.

Days of my life

OK, listen to my story. I was so happy and I wrote a nice post but before I could post it the computer stopped working like it was a frozen person. So now I am angry.

Do you want to know why I was so happy?

Because Khalid has returned home. And because last Friday, I went to my uncle's house to congratulate them about my cousin's graduation. All the family was there: my uncles, my aunts, their children and their grandchildren. There were four babies there. All of them are cute but Noor is an evil girl. From the moment she saw Sama she went to her and pushed her down. Then Aya and Medo were playing on the ground and Noor came to them and tried to attack them in every possible way.

A funny thing happened there. My mother put her food on the chair and went to take Aya from dad to feed her and sat back down on her dish. I shouted "Mooooom!" and she said in a cold voice "What?" Oh my God! Her clothes looked terrible with all that food on them. Heh heh.

Raghda slept with me in the same room. I had a good time with her. Especially at night when we talked to each other about everything. I can talk with Raghda about things I can't talk to Najma about.

Raghda fell in love with my bear toy. She slept with it and took pictures with it...I hope she enjoyed her visit.

The telephone connection between Mosul and Baghdad has been

out for six days and that is not good news. But we have Internet and we can contact our relatives there.

See you soon.

WEDNESDAY, AUGUST 3

Me again

I know that many of you thought that I had stopped posting. I was very close to that but here I am again. My mother told me not to write about politics. She said write about my normal life. But I don't have a normal life so how can I follow her advice?

Today, I left the house and was able to reach an area of Mosul that I hadn't seen for more than a year. I passed by the Lol Bridge. Yes I did. I should celebrate for that.

Aya's mom and I took Aya to kindergarten for the first time in her life. There were a lot of children there. We left Aya in a room with about eight other children and went out. All the children were crying there but me and my big sister were crying without tears. We could hear the sound of crying in the next room where we sat with the kindergarten monitor. My sister was more relaxed than I was because she couldn't recognize her daughter's voice but I was sure that the baby with the high hurting voice was Aya.

We looked at each other with fear in our faces. We waited an hour in the monitor room and went to take Aya from the small room with all the fear in it. When we came in, Aya was calm but her eyes looked smaller as if she had been crying a lot. Of course, when she saw her mother she began to cry loudly and her face looked like a tomato. She kept crying all the way to the house. Today was hard for me and Aya and her mother but it was an experiment.

Tomorrow, Aya will go again to the kindergarten but without us. She will be lonely with all those babies. Aya is the youngest baby there.

In the evening, we went to my uncle's house. His daughters came from Baghdad and we went to see his beautiful granddaughter who is five days younger than Aya. We had a good time there and afterwards we bought ice cream and came home. I don't know this feeling I am feeling now but it is a good feeling that I haven't felt for a long time.

Hmmm, I sense that my country is still beautiful in spite of everything that has happened to it.

Hadiya

WEDNESDAY, AUGUST 31

The first good thing

Hi All.

I was in Syria for about twelve days and then I went to Amman but only for two days and then I returned home to Iraq three days ago. I couldn't write because I was so busy.

First of all, when we were waiting at a checkpoint, I ran toward my dad and one American dog started barking. I stumbled and fell to the ground and twisted my ankle. My ankle swelled and became blue. My trousers tore and I looked awful. The American soldiers felt sorry for me so they bandaged my ankle. It was the first good thing that I saw the American soldiers do.

As I said I went to Syria. Syria is a beautiful Arabian country. I have never seen such a beautiful country before but I haven't visited any other country. I dream of living in Syria. Syria's people are so kind and cute. When you talk to one of them, you can feel in love and just want to hug this person. It is a nice country with nice people too. I advise you to go there someday.

Two days ago, my mom called her parents and my grandma told her my grandfather is sick so my mother left suddenly for Baghdad to take care of him. She called today to say that he is getting better and is fine.

Life outside Iraq

Hi All,

After I visited Syria and saw how the people outside of Iraq live, I can't understand why people like you read my blog when you could be doing many many things to enjoy yourselves.

Do you know one of the funny things that mom said when we went to one of Syria's cities and saw the beautiful nature there? She said, "They cheated Bush by setting up the war in Iraq."

The strange thing there in Syria, you can see a woman wearing just a little dress to cover her. And there were other women standing nearby who were completely covered and didn't show anything from their bodies. And they walked side by side and even together.

One day, we were in a shop and we heard a loud sound and we jumped. The owner of the shop asked, "You are Iraqi, huh?"

It is really strange how our countries are close but they are very different. There is no safe word in our life dictionary in Iraq. But in Syria, if you put your bag down on the street and go away, you will find it in the same place after a week.

Safety and peace are the most important things to me. So let me feel them! My mom said she hadn't seen me laugh and smile for a long time like I did in Syria. That made me think of my past life and how it was.

Every day that we spent out of Iraq, we did not come back to the hotel unless we had bought a gift for Aya. You know how much we love this baby and how much she means to us. We bought her baby books. Every day I read one to her and make her look at the pictures and I say this is "cat" and this is "dog" and I say the cat says "meow meow" and the bee says "bezzzzzz." She really likes it when I do that and laughs and smiles and her four teeth appear and make me feel a good feeling. But to keep the smile on her face, I have to reread the story again and again...

Sometimes, I wish I hadn't discovered the stories. And on the other hand, I thank God there is something called stories on this planet.

It's strange how Aya kisses the storybook all the day and she refuses to give us a kiss.

Story story, it's her only love.

WEDNESDAY, OCTOBER 12

You need to laugh

Al-salam alykum

I slept like a baby last night because I didn't have school today. My friend and I decided not to go today because (1) we didn't know how bad the situation was and (2) we didn't have an exam today. So from this hour until Monday, I will not see the light of the moon. I'm used to being in the house twenty-four hours a day.

Sometimes, I think about how much my life has changed. In the past, my dad would come back from the clinic at 10 p.m. and we would be waiting for him to go out and enjoy our night. Now he comes home at 7:30 and after 8 p.m. you can't hear the sound of feet outside.

It is something that I can't believe and when I start thinking about it, I can't stop laughing. A few days ago, I was talking about it with my mom and laughed like crazy. My sister whispered to my mother, "What is going on with this girl?" They both feared that something had happened to my mind.

You need to laugh sometimes even if it is hard to.
I am not sad right now
But I am not happy.
I am not pessimistic,
I am not optimistic,
And I am not satisfied.

I don't feel anything
And I don't expect anything either.
I want to do something,
I don't know what it is,
Just to talk to someone,
So how are you?
What is going on with you?
OK OK OK OK OK OK.
I don't mind if I write OK 100 times.
So I will not.
OK?

SATURDAY, OCTOBER 22

Questions and answers

I received several questions from Najma today. She received them from another blogger and sent me a copy so I will answer them and send a copy to another blogger and so on.

These are my answers.

Seven things I plan to do:
Read the *Arabian Nights* stories
Start a new blog in Arabic
Work on my English language skills
Try to write a book about my life
Memorize Al Quraan
Fast every Monday and Tuesday
Return to painting and writing poems

Seven things I can do:
Spend ten hours a day crying
Spend all day cooking in the kitchen
Pretend to be listening to Najma
Think of six different things at once
Spend seven days without internet connection
Spend an hour imagining
Eat a piece of food that entered Aya's mouth
    before mine.

Seven things I can't do:
Spend a day thinking about the life of the Iraqi people
Believe America
Decide what I want to be in the future
Go outside my home alone
Go outside with my family after 11 p.m.
Don't say "Oh my God!" when I see Aya
Stop eating

Seven things I say most often:
Good!
Najma, wake up!
I hate school
Mom, this is the first time you cooked tasty food like this.
Al-salam alykum
    (Peace be upon you, an Islamic greeting)
Sorry! Do you forgive me? Are you angry?
    (Every time my parents cry)
I miss Aya

Braver day by day

Boom!

Yes, I am alive.

I am writing in case you thought you would not have to read my blog anymore or hear about my un-normal life or be aware of the bad, terrible, and unacceptable situation here. I am back.

Well, life is like a ball and you are the player who can direct where the ball is going. For the last thirty days, I was feeling pessimistic, bad, angry, and afraid. But there are things around me that make me braver day by day: explosions and car bombs. I used to be afraid of them but I'm not anymore. There are other things I am afraid of. Things you don't know.

Today I am better than any day for a long while. I am laughing and smiling about the silliest things. I got my mark on the French examination and it was 42/60, a bad mark. But when I saw it I began to laugh. In usual life, if I get 90, I cry. But I think there is something in the air today, like hydrogen and nitrogen. In Iraq, there is also sadnogen and crynogen and many many gasses.

OK, I know I am silly today... But I have been really feeling bad this month. I just want to shout as loud as I can. I want to smash the ball I'm in. And I want to stop writing this post.

But I said I would write a post before I lost my mind. I did it, successfully, without calling a tear to my face.

And I spent a half an hour writing this post but then the electricity shut off. I waited for a while for the generator to come on so I could continue it. What a huge post I wrote.

How strong am I?

At the moment, I feel a little optimistic, which is unusual. We stopped going to school the day before yesterday and we rested in the house, watching TV, listening to music, and doing the things that normal people do.

Today I woke up at 9:30. Aya and the rest of my family were up, except for Najma who always sleeps late. I had my breakfast and went to study biology. The biology exam is our seventh exam! Well, you can say we go to school to get exams. The teachers in our school love to test the students. It makes us tired. I don't get enough sleep and not enough time with my family.

Some teachers see that we are tired but they don't do anything about it. They sit there and tell us how tired we look. They say we look like we are sixty years old. They tell us about their high school and how the teachers treated them... They don't get it. Our times are not their times. It seems they are still living in the past. Anyway, I didn't like school before, so how can I like it now?

I discovered that I am a strong girl. Yesterday, something fell behind our big bookcase. Well, I pushed it out to get the thing but then I couldn't push the bookcase back. My mother asked my father to do it. She told him about how I had pushed it out and he looked at me and said, "Hadiya pushed it?" "Yes, she pushed it alone," she told him. "You pushed this alone?" I said "Yes, daddy." He said, "But how could you?" "Because I am your girl."

Two days from now, it's my mom's birthday. I didn't buy her a gift because of the curfew but I will make some sweets for my great Mom.

See you soon I hope and till that time,

goodbye.

Hadiya

2006
I Want to Be Someone

Happy New Year

Happy New Year everybody. I hope in the next year we will have a real freedom that we used to dream of and still dream about. Like all the years before, 2005 came and went without making any change for the better. I feel eager to make a change in this world and for my country first—but here in Iraq dreams are just dreams. They never come true.

Sometimes I feel full of power and sometimes I feel weak. With all the explosions and all the violence around me, no one can ask why I feel such a bad feeling. Take Aya, for example. When this little girl who is one year old feels fear from the loud sounds of the explosions, she runs toward the nearest person and throws up her hands and starts beating on them to be picked up. I don't think this baby knows what violence means but she certainly realizes it is not from an angel's charity.

We are in the middle of winter. The weather in Mosul is cold and we wear all the clothes we can wear and still be able to move. The water is too cold to even wash our face in—we have to put it on the heater and then use it. One of us carries the vessel with hot water in it and pours it over the other's hands.

Because we don't have electricity most of the time during the day, we can't depend on electric heaters. In our best state, we have electricity four hours every twenty-four. But sometimes, the electricity only lasts for a half hour. Last week when the electricity went off, my sister Najma hit her head on the electric heater that we haven't been able to use yet this year. Anyway, she shouted for a flashlight and said her head was bleeding. At that time, my parents and I were sitting in the living room and there was no torch or any type of light near us. All we could tell her was to be patient until we found one. Well, thanks to Allah, she didn't hurt herself too badly.

Do you know that life with light is much easier than life without it? You can't feel happy about having something until you live without it. I have not lived a day in Iraq with continuous electricity.

The problem is our homework. We have to finish it while we have light. The generator in our neighborhood has a program—it turns on at 5 p.m. and turns off at 12 a.m. When the fuel is available.

I got good marks on my last examination but I still have a big problem with French. I have the worst marks among my friends in that subject. I really need help so if you have anything you think might help me, please send it whatever it is, a site or a song, I don't care. I want to help myself.

Oh my God! Did I write all that?

Be serious! Did you read all that?

Thank you for reading it.

And Happy New Year.

WEDNESDAY, JANUARY 4

Is it us or them?

Salam to all,
I've had a cold since yesterday. When I went to school yesterday, everybody who saw me asked: Are you asleep?

I said, I am walking and moving; how could I move if I was asleep?

Anyway, in my first period the teacher didn't come, but we got our marks ticket (report card). My marks are good except in French: as I told you I have a big, big problem with it.

I thought that we were stupid girls because each one of us pronounced the French words in a different way. But it seems that the problem is not with us. After trying five teachers I saw that each one of them pronounce the words in a different way. Every one has her own French. Nice, huh?

Today Aya and her mother visited us at lunch. Aya was too cute as usual, and she seems to love me more than Najma. Tomorrow I have an English exams. It's a strange exam. The teacher will read a paragraph twice and then ask us a few questions about it. We call this exam a "listening competition."

Good-bye now.
See you soon,
Hadiya

SUNDAY, JANUARY 29

Wartime exams

Good morning everybody. Finally I finished my midyear examinations. Yesterday I took my last exam, which was in biology. I didn't do as well on it as I wished but *Alhamdulilah* (praise God). For about twelve days, I didn't get enough sleep or enough rest. I was weak mentally and physically.

From the first days of my examinations the generator was out of order. So imagine! How could I study without light? My dad went and bought us rechargeable lights. Without them I don't know what was gonna happen to me. Especially since the electricity is still turned on for only four hours per day.

The next problem we faced was the roadblocks: most of the days the bridges were closed; the situation was bad as usual. Some days when we were in class taking our exam, we heard explosions outside. After a while we heard sounds of shooting near our building. The teachers didn't know what to do. They asked us to put our heads down and stay in place. As I said before day after day the situation is getting worse. And I am still in the middle of it.

WEDNESDAY, FEBRUARY 1
It's my life

Hi all.

Days of My Life

The holiday doesn't seem too bad. I went outside the house once so far. I am sleeping enough. I have enough time to watch TV. I can play with Aya as much as I want to.

Yesterday my friend Maas visited me. It was pleasant to see her away from school. We talked and looked at some photo albums. I had a good time with her. She was hoping to see Aya but Aya didn't visit yesterday. She came today. She is still cute but not all the time. When she wants to do something, she does it without caring if it's right or wrong. Mom often prevents her from doing whatever she wants and that makes her angry and she cries. And here we have to ignore her. That's what Supernanny said. That's hard, really hard. When she cries, my heart begins to cry with her. I can't see her tears. She is too small to carry out all the orders.

Aya found an orange the other day. She was so excited and trying to peel it with her bare hands. Of course she couldn't and so she began to weep. I turned on some music that she likes to try and make her stop weeping. As a result, Aya was crying and clapping at the same time. That was so STRANGE.

My dad often turns on the cartoons on the TV for Aya. It looks like he is used to watching cartoons. The other day, I found myself and my dad watching *Tom and Jerry* while Aya was busy doing something else.

Worries, feelings, and needs

We are going to Baghdad next Friday. I am a little worried about what is waiting for us on the road. I heard from some people that the road from Mosul to Baghdad takes about ten hours now but others say it is only six. So, it's about luck. If there are many American convoys, it will take us more time.

I am a little sad now. I went with my father to the hospital to take my big sister back home. We waited until she finished her work. It was about 6:15. For many months, I haven't been outside the house at such a late hour. The night, the moon, the streets, and the people all look different. I had a strange feeling. For just a minute, my memories came back and filled me with happiness. The radio was tuned on to an Iraqi station and was playing an Iraqi song I didn't like before today.

Before we reached the house, our neighbor called my father on the cell phone and told him that he noticed that our car was not in the garage and he was worried about what kept him late until this hour.

Are you laughing? Because sometimes when I think seriously about it, I begin to laugh until tears are falling on my cheeks.

The problem is not about the time. It's about the water, the electricity, and the danger around us. It's about our future and our history.

Many many years after 2006, Aya will come home from school crying.

Why are you crying my dear Aya?

I didn't do well on my history examination today.

Why?

The question was about the name of the leader who led Iraq for twenty years until the occupation. That is a hard question. I don't know his name.

Hi!!

Did I mention that I was going to Baghdad and the road was UN-safe??? Well, I think I did. HEY! Guess what? I'm back.

I checked my e-mail and I got ZERO new mail, which made me feel like a very important person. I can change the world in a word.

Anyway, we were lucky that the road was good. But, of course, I am tired now. I missed my bed, my computer, the Internet, and Aya. I was completely out of this world.

Tomorrow is a big day for me. I have to go to school to get my mid-examination marks. I am terrified. I am not ready. Not at all.

The driver who took us back to Mosul didn't stop talking about gas and the gasoline problems and about the price of meat. What happened to this guy? I couldn't sleep and I had a headache and I don't know what happened to my neck. I can't move it easily. My body is angry now.

Your only hope in the world.

Hadiya

TUESDAY, FEBRUARY 21

A part of my life's diary

I am sorry. I know I am late. This time it's not my fault. I couldn't find time to write a post. I know that you are waiting to hear any news about my marks. OK, I got good marks in Math, Physics, Chemistry, English, Islam, and Arabic. But in Biology, I got the lowest marks I ever got in my life. 81! On the other hand, I got 91 in French. I need to get 95 on my next test so I don't have to take the final examination.

When I was answering the questions in the Math exam I began to cry because I was feeling afraid and I answered wrong. I didn't have enough time to answer it right so I wrote the wrong numbers. There was a teacher there who knows what a state I get into during exams. She came to me and said, "Relax, Hadiya, relax please. I will bring water to you. Don't cry or be worried. It's OK if you get 99 instead of 100." Blah blah. Her speech made me cry more. She always makes me cry during the exam. But the good news is that I got 99.

The situation is still getting worse. There were sounds of shelling last night. It makes me feel angry. I just wanted to sleep. I wish that I had something to cover my ears whenever I don't want to hear the sounds around me.

The only thing that makes me feel happy is Aya. I made a mistake yesterday when I drew a picture of a cartoon for her. She loved my drawing and wanted me to draw more but I had to go to sleep. She began to cry and yell and was walking behind me with a pen and a piece of paper and shouting in baby talk. After a long war between the two of us, we went to sleep.

See ya. E-mail me.

FRIDAY, FEB 24
Without comment

Twinkle twinkle, my darkness life,
Let me see the headlines.
I am hurting because I am blind.
    I am sad and I don't know why. It's not because I can't find a reason to feel like I do but because I don't know which reasons have covered my life with all this pain. Every second makes me weaker.

With all the pressures in school, with all the bombs, I don't know what to do. What to say?!? I don't like sitting here in this place watching people killing each other, cheating each other, and fighting each other.

I can swear that this war has changed my life 180 degrees. I am sixteen years old. I should be living the happiest part of my life. I should be a crazy girl doing foolish and stupid things but I am not. I am talking like someone who is thirty-five. I feel I am nothing. I do nothing in my life and I am going to do nothing.

My friend's brother is very ill. Nine days ago, he woke up and he couldn't see anything. Now he is blind and cannot speak. He has a headache all the time. He gets worse and worse each day. The doctors don't know what happened to him. They gave him drugs but his body didn't respond. In Iraq, there is no hope of survival. My friend's family is trying to get out of the country. Maybe they will find an answer to his condition in some other country.

Have you ever wanted to disappear?

Have you ever wanted to scream?

Have you ever felt that you are being led by something outside yourself? Well, I am.

The electricity is better now. It comes on for about twelve hours. But the generator crashed so we still have to live twelve hours each day without electricity. I've lived twenty hours and even twenty-four without it but I am sick of it. If that's all that America can give the Iraqi people—12 hours of electricity—why did they come here?

In the morning, I study on the roof of our house. The sunlight is a good friend to me these days. Najma and I were studying on the roof yesterday and there were many helicopters flying in the air around our house. Najma hopes that they will shoot us so that we will not have to study because then we will be in heaven playing. That's what she said yesterday. But in Iraq, no dream will come true, thank God.

Look! Can you hear the sound of the helicopters? It seems that they hear us talking about them.

XXXXXXXXX
XXXX Hadiya XX
XXXXXXXXX

SATURDAY, MARCH 11

Two days in hell

Three days ago, our first day in hell started when my mother answered the phone and talked with my aunt. My aunt told my mother that my father's uncle was killed that day by bullets from an American soldier. The police called my cousin who was going to have her engagement party the next day. They asked if she knew someone named "S"? She told them that she knew him very well so they said he was injured and taken to hospital. My cousin began to cry and yell and told her parents what the police told her. My aunt and her husband went at once to the hospital and found that "S" had died. My aunt's husband told the American soldiers that Uncle "S" is an old man, seventy-eight years old and it was clear he was not a terrorist. The soldiers told him that they were sorry.

Uncle "S" didn't die because he was seventy-eight years old. Not even because he lived fifty years with only one kidney. And not because he was tired from raising his children after his wife's death. Uncle "S" died because an American soldier shot him. He died on the same day as his brother had died, March 8th. I didn't cry that day. I couldn't study or go to sleep like a human. I couldn't do anything. I just sat here thinking what next? The next was in the next day.

In the morning, we didn't go to school at the usual time because Aya was in a bad temper and she didn't want to go to the nursery. When we got to my school around 7:45, the windows were broken, the girls were crying, and the teachers were in a panic. Some of the girls were running, others were talking, and the rest were crying. Everything looked strange. My friend Maas was the first one I talked to. She told me that a mortar fell on our school garden.

After then, the police came. Some of them went up to the roof and the rest stayed in the garden and the schoolyard. You don't know how much the girls felt at peace when they saw the police.

Now the girls that weren't crying before, cried this time. And when we finally helped one girl to feel better and stop crying, another girl would start to cry and so on.

As you know, it's not legal to have a cell phone in school—only the teachers can have them. This was the time when we really needed our cell phones especially because the police said there was another bomb that didn't explode yet.

With the help of Allah, we found a girl who brought her mobile with her that day. I used it to call my father and asked him to come and take us home. I cried when I talked to him because I couldn't stand any more pain. My father came to school and took me and my sister to our home.

And yesterday too was a very bad day. It began with the news that my friend's father died of cancer and ended with a car bombing in our neighborhood. The explosion was so big that I thought I died and then returned to life. And because I am alive, I write this post.

SUNDAY, MARCH 24

Explosions and examinations

First of all, I want to thank everyone who wrote a comment or a letter. I read them all but I couldn't find time to answer.

This week was like all the weeks before, full of explosions and examinations. I didn't have my French examination yet so I need your prayers, a big big prayer.

Believe it or not, we went outside. My father took us to al-Sada. I hadn't been in that place for many long months.

I feel bored talking about the situation and the dangers we pass through so I want to show you a small essay I wrote two or three years ago. My English teacher asked us to write them then and she only returned them this week. All of us were laughing at ourselves. You can't imagine how bad our English was. Laugh as much as you want. Now I leave you with my essay.

> In the holiday, I was going to the north of Iraq. I saw the magic nature which I believe is the communication between the God and the people. I felt very excited when I see it. After that, I was going to my family house. I was missing my other family. Therefore, I was leaving for Baghdad. I saw what the enemy destroyed. I went back home and was working on some things. The holiday is ended and the school is beginning. I am very sad about that.

You have to feel lucky that I hadn't begun blogging at that time. My English teacher had asked us to write an essay about any subject we like. But nobody wrote anything. My friend told the teacher that she couldn't find a subject to write about. So the teacher told her to write an essay about how much she suffered to find a subject to write about.

What do you want me to write about? I feel empty and I don't want to talk about the situation or about the war (three years of war) because I know I will burst into tears when I do.

SATURDAY, APRIL 8

The worst day in Iraq

First and foremost, the same reasons as before prevented me from posting for the last two weeks: I was full of exams. Anyway, I'm OK now because Aya is here and she will paint smiles on our faces as she always does. She will entertain us with her actions all the day. I came up with one thing: There is no one in my family that I can stand to be without more than Aya. I love her so much. I think I love her more than I have to. I don't think I will ever love somebody more than I love Aya right now.

I am doing well in school. But the next two weeks will not be easy ones.

We will not go to school tomorrow. Does the date April 9th remind you of anything? It reminds me of the worst day in Iraq. The worst day that every single Iraqi lived. In the beginning, there were some people who loved the U.S. Army and believed that they came to help us but now, after three years have passed, there is nobody that believes that anymore, nobody who hasn't lost someone from their family or someone they loved.

Last week, we went to the north of Iraq, to Duhuk. We had a good time there and took many pictures. We took Aya to "Dream City" but she refused to play any of the games. We tried and tried to make her play. We know that she had never visited a "Dream City" before and we thought she would have a good time there, but it seems we were wrong.

THURSDAY, APRIL 27

A new day with a new outlook

Hello, everybody, I miss you too.

About my school and my marks, I did very well in French (66/60,

66/70) and biology (100, 100, 100, 92). I really did my best and thank God, I got the best marks.

The students who got more than 90 percent in all subjects will not go to school until the next term.

Today we had a little party in the school but not a good one. Some of the girls had examinations and the others were busy with their marks. But I had a good time with my friends and I took some pictures with them. Every one of us cooked something or brought something to eat. Gathering around the table and eating together is nice. Do you know that feeling when you love all human beings?

You're right that I finished my school and my examinations but I still have to study for the sixth grade [senior year of high school] a year before the school begins. This year will be very important to us. It will decide our fate. So today I went for my first period course in chemistry. The chemistry teacher is a man. In our school, until now, all our teachers were women so we are not used to this. Now we have to be polite and good students. It's hard for me, you know. In our school, we are all girls. We jump and cry and do whatever we want. We are free.

Now I want to go and read a story. Guess what its name is? It's a Harry Potter story! I can't wait to read it, so, bye! I will talk to you later, maybe tomorrow.

SATURDAY, APRIL 29

The conversation between reality and imagination

Good morning.

Today I am going to post my essay that I wrote a week ago. My English teacher asked us to write an essay about whatever we wanted and express our thoughts and our dreams in this essay. The title of my subject is:

THE CONVERSATION BETWEEN REALITY AND IMAGINATION

Alaa Al-din took me on his magic carpet to the sky.

I told him that I was dreaming of living at that height.

He thought deeply and said you are the leader in your life.

I told him the doors were all locked inside my eyes.

He stood silent and then said you did not try to open the doors, you have never tried.

I told him that I tried but I lied and lied and lied.

The expression of sadness was drawn in his eyes. He said you don't have enough confidence in your life and he was right. I admit that he was right.

I told him I was scared like a mouse in the night.

He told me that I can't get what I want without a fight.

I told him that the enemy was large in size and I didn't have the courage to face him and so I cried.

He told me that I was like the prince in the chess game and I belonged to the blue side.

I told him there is no prince in chess and there are only two sides, the black and white.

He said you choose to be like the queen but you don't play that part in your life. You chose to play for no side and you are really blind.

I told him that I lied to him, that I knock on the door but when it opens, I hide.

His eyes began to glow. He said you didn't take any step in your life. Your soul was not a home. You chose to live the other's life.

He touched my hand and said in the center of your black eyes, there is a light. If you want to catch it, you have to fight.

My dear, you have to fight.

The teacher arranged a seminar between the students. Each girl read the essay she wrote in front of the teachers and the other girls. And there were many good essays and mine was one of them. At the end of the seminar, the teacher awarded the two girls who had written the best two essays and I was one of the winners. The teacher gave us an album as a gift. I was so surprised because I didn't expect this. But I was happy too.

I will stop writing now and leave the other news for another day.

MONDAY, MAY 1

I want to be someone...

Good morning. Good evening. Good night. It's not important which time I use as much as it's important that it is good.

I went to my first period course in chemistry. The teacher was so nice to us. He didn't stop joking and doing funny things. I laughed and laughed—more than I have laughed this whole year. My tears began to fall and I didn't know what to do... In physics, my teacher is a woman who seems like a good teacher too. The subjects don't look easy, but nothing is hard if we study hard.

I still don't know what I want to be in the future. Before, I hoped to be a pharmacist just like my aunt. But now I changed my mind. I like house decoration but there are no colleges for studying decorations. I don't know if I want to be someone famous. I want to enter an excellent college somewhere far from the Iraqi situation. I want to leave Iraq and study and come back to my country when I am ready for that. And at that time, I will do for my country and give and give all that I have just to see it rise as high as it was in the past.

I don't know why my mother always says Najma is an ambitious person who has confidence and dreams bigger than herself. And me? I am nothing at all. Oh, she didn't say I was nothing at all but that's what she meant when she was talking. She said Najma is a very good English speaker and she is very good on the computer and blah blah blah. And when she finished, she turned her head to me and said "You are good, too." Did she really think I don't feel that? I am not blind. I am the only daughter she has who doesn't wear eyeglasses.

That's exactly what I want to prove. I want to prove that I am not the girl she thinks I am. I also have dreams, I also have plans. But I also have something Najma does not—I'm afraid of everything.

I have fears of building hopes on no foundation. I have fears from listening to myself and getting into trouble. I hate myself sometimes just like I do now. I hate sitting with people I hate because it's too clear I hate them and now I am sitting with me and I hate myself just now. Not a good condition to talk about. Better to leave myself now.

THURSDAY, MAY 4

Another flower opens in my family tree

Hello all.

My father went to France last week and he will remain there for about one month. I miss him already and so does Aya. She doesn't stop asking where he is. When he first left the house, she wouldn't stop crying and so we told her he had gone to the mosque to pray. She saved that information in her mind and now whenever we mention his name, she remembers that Lalli is praying. I don't know why his prayer takes so long.

We are only five women in the house—my mother, my big sister, Aya, Najma, and me. But today a lovely man joined us. So that we will not be scared or something, we have a man in the house.

Ladies and gentleman, I introduce you to our man:

His name is Ayman.

His age: 21 hours.

His look: Very little pale baby with some blonde hair and small miserable eyes. He is cute, calm, and skinny.

Until the last day, I did not believe that a baby would come into our lives and join our family. I don't blame Aya for not expecting this even after all our trying to make her ready for it and not jealous.

The first time I saw my nephew, I said he's too tiny. He is really too tiny. His face is much smaller than the palm of my hand. But for Aya, he is a big boy who might steal his mother's heart. When Aya first saw him, she said "Baby, Baby, Baby, Baby, Baby, Baby...

She said that more than thirty times.

When Aya's father told her that Ayman is crying because he is hungry, she rushed to her room where she left her bottle and went quickly to him and tried to feed him. We gave Aya new toys and told her that the baby had given them to her and that somehow helped.

The first hours after their meeting were UNbelievable. Whenever Ayman stopped crying, Aya started to cry, and so on. You can say we had a crying party in our house. But now Aya feels much better than before. I hope she will love him...

Yours, Aunt Hadiya

SATURDAY, MAY 6

Ayman says...

Hello, my name is Ayman. I am now three days old. I have one sister who seems very kind to me. Especially because I am the only one who is being kissed by her. I

give her a gift every day to make her love me and not be jealous.

She cried when she saw them give me a bath. The first day was full of tears for her. Whenever I stopped crying, she began to cry.

She calls me "Amony" (I like this name) and when she said "Amony," all the family forgot who Amony is and the only cute baby they remembered is Aya. I don't blame them. She is more beautiful than I am. She walks and talks and does things that makes the whole family laugh.

Today, I saw her eating a cucumber after she dipped it in the cola. I wonder if that tastes good.

Anyway, I love my family but I haven't seen my grandfather yet, I heard them talking on the phone and they said he is in France. They said in France, there are streets and lights and other things. I hope that when my grandfather comes back from France, he will love me as much as he loves Aya.

I sleep almost all day. They think I don't want to play with them because they left me and went to play with Aya.

OK, bye now, I have to sleep before the night falls. Because my hope is not to let my mother sleep when it is night. That's fun. Try it!

Talk to you later.

WEDNESDAY, MAY 17

Secret doors and silly Hadiya

A part of my heart is feeling very grateful to my mom and dad. My mother took us to buy some clothes and other things today. As I mentioned before, my father is in France and he contacts us every day. He is doing well. He said he put on some weight and he is enjoying his time and wishes that we were with him. He said he couldn't buy any gifts for us because the price is too high there. And so my mom is buying gifts for us from Iraq and we will pretend that these clothes are from France. Who says otherwise?

The other part of my heart is feeling that it is missing somebody. I miss my dad. I want him sitting right here beside me. I miss Ayman so much—I haven't seen him since last Saturday. I don't know why I am missing him so much. He doesn't say a word or do something that makes me fall in love. He doesn't open his eyes and look at me.

He doesn't beat me or push me or do the stuff Aya does to me. But I miss him. I'm beginning to forget what he looks like.

Yesterday my mother and I went to the tiny market in our neighborhood but it was closed, so we changed direction and went to this super tiny market and bought the things we needed. But when we were going to our house, we saw that the first tiny market was open so we entered and saw one of our neighbors there. The neighbor asked my mother how my father was and she told him that he's fine and our neighbor said of course he is fine because he is far away from the explosions and the bullets.

Just then, we heard a loud explosion of bullets and I didn't know what was happening outside. The shopkeeper told us to go to a safer place in the market but that wasn't working. It was clear the bullets were in the street. So he held his phone and called his mother and asked her to open the door and we ran to her house.

But where is the door???

Do you know the story of Alice in Wonderland? When she became small, she opened a door and went inside. Anyway, the door he asked his mother to open was that size. I didn't know if I could pull myself through that door, which led to the garden. We sat at his house for a while and then went back home.

I don't care what size the door was, it was a very good door. As they say, don't judge a book by its cover. I don't know who said that but I know I say don't judge the door by its size.

He he. How silly am I???

If you are with people who say that I am silly, come to Iraq and live for months and we will see. Will the silly life here make you silly or not?

FRIDAY, MAY 19

The best picture I have ever drawn

MONDAY, MAY 22

Just like a ghost

I woke up today and told my mother I am not feeling OK. I didn't eat my breakfast or my lunch because I have a pain in my abdomen and I couldn't look at my food. It's hard to explain BUT the last two months, I lost eight pounds. I look awful now, just like a ghost. My mom doesn't like the way I look at all. She often uses these words: "when you were pretty..." Well, she means I am ugly right now. There is no other way to explain her words.

Anyway, I am trying to get my weight back and I ate so much yesterday. I eat everything that I see. So now you know why I am sick today...

WEDNESDAY, MAY 24

It's a star, it's...

Aya came today. She prevents us from touching or sitting by Ayman. She says "Mal Mamia!" She means that he is her mother's baby. She still thinks that my father is praying. I don't think praying needs all that time, really. Anyway, she took the phone and said to him "Gagawa Laali," which means "Grandfather, please come here." I am eager to see my father but I am more eager to see the meeting between Aya and my father. I am sure they are both missing each other very much.

I had a terrible night. I closed my eyes and when I was so close to being in my first nightmare, the electricity turned off. Now I lived the nightmare. It was too hot and besides there are many mosquitoes this summer. What's the problem?

I opened the window and looked to the sky between the wires and I could see the stars. Oh, the star lights for a minute and stops after a while. Oh, it's moving! Oh, it's a helicopter! Sorry...

Just imagine my night with the noise of helicopters and generators. A very beautiful night!

FRIDAY, MAY 26

Food!!

Maybe we don't have electricity, peace, and freedom but we certainly have food. Maybe we can't drive, walk, and do the simple, normal things, but we can eat.

Aya on Najma's birthday

This is *klaiga* before baking. Iraqi people usually make this sweet before Eid.

Klaiga ready to be eaten.

The donuts I make are some of the best donuts ever....but the cheesecake I make is the worst cheesecake ever.

In order to survive

"In order to survive, human beings have to cooperate. And in order to cooperate, they have to communicate their ideas, feelings, and needs."

The paragraph above is one of the subjects included in my English book for the fifth grade [the Iraqi equivalent of a high school junior in American schools]. So in order for me to survive, I will communicate.

1. My ideas

I am thinking right now about how I will be able to live next month. They said the government will cut Mosul off from electricity for fifteen days. Fifteen days without electricity? Are they kidding???

2. My feelings

My feelings. I am feeling pessimistic right now. I went to take my physics period and when I was getting back home, I saw about three tanks, the large-sized ones. At the same time, there were two helicopters flying above my head. It's not a good feeling when you see that. When a tank or any kind of U.S. soldiers' vehicles are in the street, all the cars drive behind them about twelve miles an hour.

As I said, I have lost so much weight this month. Today, I was wearing my gold ring and suddenly I felt there was something missing. I looked at my finger and it wasn't there. I rushed around looking for it and tried to remember all my movements. Well, it worked. I found it.

Do you know what? I am sixteen going on seventeen. I will be seventeen next week on the 3rd of June. I will be wiser, taller, thinner, and perhaps uglier than the year before.

Now it's my time for watching TV.

SUNDAY, JUNE 11

What I want

My birthday was seven days ago but I didn't find time to write about it until now.

My birthday was not a good day. Maybe it was the worst birthday I ever had. There wasn't a birthday party or a birthday cake or any sweets. I didn't even have to brush my teeth before I went to bed. Am I feeling happy with these seventeen years in my life? NOT AT ALL!

It's a miserable feeling. I always want the time to go faster and I always want the year to go by as fast as possible. But when I see that the year has really passed and nothing has changed in reality, I feel very angry and guilty.

I feel guilty when I smile—a smile has become something UNusual in our lives because I know that in this moment, the lives of many families are destroyed. Many kids are losing their parents and many wives have become widows. I feel guilty because I shut my mouth and watch this horrible movie come alive. I am guilty because I have already accepted to live and act in this movie. I feel guilty because in my past life I thought this problem would be solved by playing a part in the movie. I feel guilty because I am guilty.

A few days ago, Najma asked why I looked so sad. She said, "If you will cry, don't answer." Well, I didn't. Then she asked me, "Do you want to get out of Iraq?"

My real option and only choice is that I want to stay in Iraq. I want to see Iraq shining again. I am not sure that I will but I am sure that I will stay.

Events of a week

Yesterday I was going to write a new post but I ended up drawing a picture with some tears in my eyes. In front of my aunt's house, a booby-trapped car exploded last week. All the windows and all the doors and most of the walls crashed in...most of the family went to the hospital and they are OK now. NOBODY DIED and that is something we are grateful for.

Two days ago, an eleven-year-old child living near our house was injured by bullets when he was in his father's car. They took him to the hospital at once, but he died. Also my friend's cousin was killed last week in Baghdad...and a blast fell on my uncle's house.

Big explosions were heard around here the last few weeks. The last one ended with the whole family shouting, "Najmaaaa!" and she shouted back "Alive!" and then all things returned as they were, just because we have to go on in this life. We have a huge reason to not want to live, but we live and go on in this life. So many people wanted to live. They wanted to fight to stay alive but they couldn't live.

The question

I know it has been so long since I wrote my last post. I know that you were worried about me and that you are sorry about what is going on in Iraq. I know all that because I hear it over and over again as if I was wearing your shoes and forget that I am the one who is living this life and I feel sorry for my poor wounded soul.

I wish the reason for not writing a new post was that I was busy with my lessons or with Aya and Ayman. But it's not. Right now, I consider myself half human.

All days are the same, just like the other days repeating themselves. Wake up early, have my breakfast, and study, study, study until it is time for my class and after that I get back and study all over again. The same program is running my life and I would accept if it means that the killing, bombing, and stealing does not go on too.

I have spent bad and hard days since I wrote my last post. The situation is deteriorating rapidly. I don't know where to start. Many things happened and I can't number them. But here is an example:

My dad went to work with my big sister—Aya was with them in the car—when they heard the sound of bullets being fired at the tanks of the U.S. soldiers. The tanks were in front of my father's car on the other side of the road. My father's car was not the only one there. Anyway, after the shooting stopped, the soldiers got crazy like they always do.

They ordered the people sitting in the cars to get out and put their hands on their heads. The soldiers threw out everything from my father's pockets. My father asked the soldiers to send Aya and her mother to the car because it was too hot. They didn't even try to listen to him. They shouted loudly and didn't accept his word. But the Iraqi police told my sister she could go to the car, although she would have to keep the doors open.

My sister sat in the car with my little niece Aya who was shouting for my father. She was crying, probably because she was thirsty. My sister was afraid to move and open her bag to get the water out. You can't guess what the soldiers' reaction would be to that. She stayed in her place thinking about my father. What was he feeling? Was he thirsty? She was worried about his state because my father has had a heart attack. It's not good for normal people to be in that situation so what about a sixty-year-old man? She was cursing the soldiers silently. What a humiliation for a respectable man.

The situation continued for an hour and a half but for some people, like my sister, it seemed like a year.

When he returned home, my dad said nothing. My sister said, "Do you know what happened to us today?" My father interrupted and said, "Nothing happened to us." She told the story anyway and my father didn't comment. He picked up his glass and was drinking his water like he always does, trying not to make us feel worried.

It takes a strong man like my father to forget these things. I am not a man and I am not strong. When danger is around me or my family or my friend, I can't sit watching. This is not only a war against Saddam or terrorism—it is a war against us. It is a psychological war.

To live or not to live. That is the question.

Bye-bye peace of mind. See you in heaven. Maybe.

FRIDAY, JULY 28

The Victims

When the victims are...
When the victims
Are your uncles
Who built our future
Who gave us life
Our hopes die
When they die.
They are the victims
Of this war.

A couple of days ago, I was sitting with my family watching TV. About 11:30, I went to bed and I noticed that I had an unread message on my mobile phone. It was from my friend Maas. I thought it might be a normal message, a joke or something like that. But I read the message and it said, "My family is in a horrible state. My uncle was killed this morning when he was coming home from the mosque in Baghdad." The feeling that I felt that moment I can't describe. I rushed downstairs and told my parents and then I went to my bedroom and cried for a long time. I feel very sorry for Maas. She was so busy this month. She went to Baghdad to do an extra examination. When the victim is your family...

Danger surrounds us all the time but this time was not the same. Hearing the sounds of bombs is something that we are used to so we don't disturb ourselves and stop what we are doing just because of the sound of a bomb. But this time when my father's phone rang it was my uncle and he told my father that two mortars had fallen on the roof of his house. He was sleeping and little pieces of the roof fell on his bed and the floor. His wife was not aware that the mortars had fallen on their own house. She went to my uncle's room and found him sitting on his bed holding pieces of stone.

And when the victim is your family...

A new day came and a car bomb exploded in front of my relatives' house. All the windows and all the doors were broken. The explosion was very close to their house and it was very big. Three of my relatives were injured and moved to the hospital. They are OK now, but many people lost their lives because of that car bomb.

At the beginning of the war, when we heard an explosion we called all the family to make sure that they are fine. But now because the explosions don't stop all day, we stopped calling each other. But when the explosion hurts someone from your family, the victim is you.

When the victim is you.
Our souls live in our hearts.
Our hearts are inside our bodies.
Our bodies live in our homes.
Our homes are our country.
Our county has been destroyed.
We are the victims of this war.

I consider all people living in Iraq victims. And I am a victim too because I am living in Iraq. I am a victim because no day passes without hurting me in some way or another. I am a victim because every day makes me weaker. I am a victim now because I will be a victim sooner or later. The people who are killed and who die, they have left Iraq and their suffering. But we? We are still suffering and we are waiting our turn to die and leave Iraq.

When the victim is your niece...

Iraqi children are the victims of this war. Aya is a victim of this war. What else would you call a child of one year and a half living in these conditions? Could you find a baby of that age who knows what a generator is? When the electricity is turned off, she begins to cry and shout for the generator—"Generator, please turn on!" Isn't she the real victim of this war?

No wonder that one of her first words was, "It's hot." How sad it is to see her suffering. When the electricity is turned off, Aya stands in front of the fan and says the weather is hot. The look on her face expresses her needs. Her needs are not easy to get but so easy to lose.

In June, Hadiya began corresponding with Sasha Crow, a Human Shield in Baghdad when the war began, and cofounder of the Collateral Repair Project, working with refugees both inside and outside of Iraq.

JULY 30 CHAT

Sasha: Do you wear the hijab?

Hadiya: Yes, I wear the hijab. I do it because I want to. In fact, I wore it before I was supposed to and before my parents asked me to.

Sasha: I have a man friend in Amman who told me that women are more beautiful in a hijab—that the eyes show the soul and when all you see is mostly eyes, you see a woman's true beauty...

Hadiya: Maybe I will send you my picture sometime—but I won't send you one of me because I am ugly now...

Sasha: Ah Hadiya—I doubt that you are ugly. Your words are beautiful—like eyes they show the soul...

Hadiya: I put this thing—I don't know what you call it. It's something to put in the mouth...

Sasha: Is it for straightening your teeth? Braces?

Hadiya: It really hurts me, I lost five kilos (11 pounds) because I put it in my mouth three months ago. The doctor said I need to wear them for one and a half years. I hope I can take them off before I go to college!

Sasha: That is a long time. When you get them out, you will not remember what you looked like without them...

AUGUST 9
The Poem

Reach the sky or touch the ground.
The earth is always moving around.
When the curfew started,
I felt the earth stop moving around.
At that time, I could feel the wind,
I could see the hand of the clock moving

But still I think the earth
Has stopped moving around.
Many answers cannot be found.
I know it's impossible for this to happen
But it did happen before
When the earth was moving,
And the time was running,
When I was frozen to the ground.
I was scared to take my breath,
I was afraid to act like a hero
And go on with my life.
It's not as easy as it sounds.
It sounds like every movement
Makes an improvement.
It sounds like peace will soon be found
It sounds like we are the leaders of our lives,
It sounds like they are working on our account.
It sounds like we are all the evils
And they are God's angels.
It sounds like their soldiers are not armed.
Their words, their lies
Are the fence we are surrounded by.
We are surrounded by their arms
By their tanks,
By their violence.
They did nothing
To make their mothers proud.
Sleeping was my only option

To escape from reality
But my plan fell through
When the explosion woke me up.
It sounded like it was really loud.
Now I know that hope will come
Not when I will be asleep
But when the earth
Stops moving around.

AUGUST 9 CHAT

Hadiya: No one really understands what is really happening here. Last week, one of our relatives was kidnapped...

Sasha: Oh no! Are they home now?

Hadiya: Yes, he paid soooo much money and they released him...

Sasha: Oh that is horrid! I am so glad he's OK—of course, there is no price for someone you love so it is worth the money. But it is still horrid...

Hadiya: I don't know. Sometimes we think seriously of getting out of Iraq but it is hard to leave your house and your family. My parents worked so hard to build this house...

Sasha: Everyone I know there has either left or is preparing to leave. It is the hardest decision...

Hadiya: Sometimes we say it doesn't matter if we leave. The most important thing is to feel peace—but does peace really exist?

TUESDAY, SEPTEMBER 7

The night and the light

I have been disconnected from my blog for the last few weeks because I was in Syria. After my father finally decided there was no hope of living a normal life here and we couldn't get any fuel from the fuel station, he gave the order for us to travel to Syria.

I visited Syria once before but most of all I was eager and excited to leave Iraq. Well, I think if they took me to the desert I would be happy to be far away from the bombs and the bullets.

Our trip was hard and exhausting. We needed fourteen hours to reach Aleppo. We spent four hours in the immigration and passport center. As you can see in the picture, there are hundreds of people waiting to hear their names called and get their passport and go back

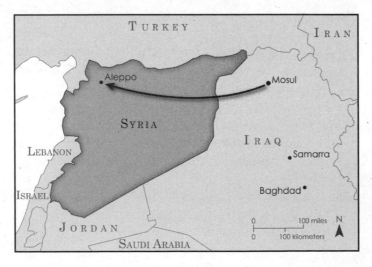

to their cars to continue their trip.

We reached Aleppo at 11 at night. It was the first time I could see the night since we were in Syria last year. Do you know why I love Syria? Because I can see the night. I can see the black sky, which I never liked until now.

I love Syria because here you can see many people walking in the street with no fear—and guess what? They are smiling too. I love Syria because the policemen do not show their arms here.

I love Syria because here the people know what freedom means. I love Syria because in Syria there are green trees and happy children and a real life. I love Syria because here simple families live a simple life far from violence...

I am not sure that I am happy to return home. The only thing I missed when I was in Syria were my sister and her children and our bathroom.

Hey, I went to Syria for ten days and while we were gone, the government remembered for the first time that there are students working hard and studying in the dark. The government did its best not to forget that they are human beings and that human beings have to improve themselves and their skills. The government remembered the students who sit up all night and study by the light of candles feeling so cold and unable to focus while the shooting takes place in the neighborhood. They finally remembered the students who went to their schools and left their mothers in the house worried about them and praying that they will come back home safe.

Hey, they remembered the people who will build the future and yes, these people are the babies who will grow up and learn to write and speak in English. These babies become teenagers. These teenagers have sites on the Internet now and they are writing about the government's work.

You know what the government did? It turned on the electricity!

Can you share my happiness and sit up and clap your hands? Although I missed all this because I was in Syria, I am happy that the government remembered me. Thank you all for listening.

SEPTEMBER 17 CHAT

Hadiya: Hi Sasha. How are you? I am too busy. I have a small party here tomorrow. My friends and my sister's friends will come to our house because my sister finished her high school and now she is going to go to college. Here are some answers to your questions...

I guess I started writing my blog to tell the people about what is going on in this war. I have been writing my diary in a small copybook since I was twelve so I'm used to writing about my life. It is a way to translate my anger into words. Reading my diary for the last five years reminds me of the people I love and the simple dreams that came true and my old-fashioned thoughts.

Sasha: When you were a young girl what did you want to be when you grew up? Can you remember why you wanted to do these things?

Hadiya: I wanted to be a singer. I was looking to have a nice voice like Fayrouz. I used to hear her songs on the radio in the morning and they were refreshing to my mind. I wanted to be a musician because I have a musician's ears.

Then I wanted to be a teacher because I loved my teachers and they loved me too. And guess what? I wanted to be a writer and, well, I still dream of opening a big library in Mosul.

One day, I was searching for some books in our bookcase and in many of the books I opened, I found an acknowledgement from the writer and guess what? The writer was my grandfather! Finally, I opened a book and found some words written for my mother from my grandpa and it said, "My dear daughter. I give you this book so that maybe you will continue the work that I started."

So I guess that made me feel I wanted to be someone that my grandfather will be proud of...

Sasha: Who is your hero or heroine? Why?

Hadiya: I think both of my grandfathers are my heroes and my father as well. They always talk about the love that mothers have in their hearts for their children. But my father has that much love and more. When I am with my father, I feel peace because I am sure he will do anything to protect me. He is my hero because he makes me feel peace in the middle of war...

Hadiya's Diary

A new day has come

Salaam to all.

There is no argument that I had fun in Syria and this journey helped me to redraw the smile on my face. But it also made me feel that the seventeen years I have lived are all in vain.

Honestly, when I reached Syria I told Najma well, it's OK—it's only seventeen years. But hey!! That's all of my life.

There were so many questions dancing and moving in a circle and making a noise in my mind. What was I doing these seventeen years? How could I forget this? I was studying history when I realized that it contains so many lies and little truth.

I don't say that I haven't done anything in those seventeen years, but the things I did are not helpful. Anyway, I woke up from my last life and maybe now I am going somewhere. So I came from Syria carrying hopes and dreams of a future.

But when we were finally home, there was a car preparing itself for suicide and it exploded near our house. We didn't lose any of our windows but some neighbors did and died exploded.

Well, after another car bomb and after the daily small explosions and bullets, I am still carrying hopes that I will find hope someday.

Another day started when I heard that one of our relatives had been killed. I tried to forget this as usual and I think I must have succeeded because I haven't talked about since the sun's rays fell below the horizon.

I have had really bad nightmares the last few days but today, I didn't see anything when I was asleep. Seeing nothing is better than the nightmares certainly.

There is hot news. Our telephone was repaired this morning. It has not been working since the 9th of January. It was so long since then that I even forgot how to use it. But after a while, I called my grandma and when she answered, my tone changed automatically to a child's voice. I could hardly hold back my tears. I really really miss my grandparents and I can't wait to see them again.

My school will start tomorrow and here we go into our last year in high school. College, I can't wait to see you.

FRIDAY, SEPTEMBER 29
Ramadan Kareem (the Generous Month)

Al-salaam alykum,

First of all, I returned to school and began the fight with studying. I am scared about this year. I have to get high marks to enter a college that is suitable for me. I need to put in more effort and study more.

Well, this photo shows our breakfast on the first day of Ramadan.

I love Ramadan. I think the best days that I have lived are during Ramadan, especially before the war. Ramadan was unbelievable for me. Ramadan made me feel happy more than anything else. I can't understand why. When I don't eat anything for fourteen hours I am supposed to feel hungry and angry too. But when I feel hungry during Ramadan, I smile and am really happy. Ramadan gives us joy...

THURSDAY, OCTOBER 12
Home, school, and between...

Salaam alykum

I have no excuse for not writing. I have been really busy and had no time to write. Since school started, I spend five hours a day studying and I hardly have time to chat with my family.

Well, when I come home from school, I open my mouth and don't close it. I mean I talk so much about what's going on with me. But I don't listen.

I usually go to bed and only need to put my head down on my pillow to fall asleep and after having a nap for an hour, I wake up and study for two more hours and then another three or four hours after breakfast. The only spare time I have is when I watch TV and read a few pages from Harry Potter's story before I go back to sleep.

This school year is not like every year because we will go to college next year. Me in college? NO WAY! I just entered primary school yesterday and now they want to put me in a college!

I was so surprised this year when I heard that two girls from my class got married and another two got engaged. And here I have to stop and shout. Am I the only one who still has a pink room with bears on her bed and Barbie toys in her drawer? And I'm not sure that if I find them I won't play with them. I am not a little girl anymore and I am not a woman. I am in between.

I had a good time with Aya today who is now speaking and controlling us. We spent fifteen minutes sitting in a circle—me and Najma and Aya and my mom—just doing what Aya asked us to do.

Aya will sleep in our house tonight. Her mother called and asked us not to bring her home because there was a shooting and as she described it, "a small battle" near her house. Her house is really near ours: I don't know why we didn't hear anything. Anyway, a minute later, a cousin called and said there was another "small battle" near her house and wanted to know if there was fighting where we live.

Well, we turned off the light in the sitting room and Aya was shouting, "It's danger, Grandpa, come inside it's danger!" So we moved to another room and turned on the TV and played with Aya who began to cry when she heard her mother's voice on the telephone.

When Aya was born, I thought I had finally found someone to tell what to do and what not to do. But I was wrong. Aya shouted at me twice today and gave orders and told ME what to do. She yelled at me, "Stop bothering us!" The only thing I was doing was talking. Is that a crime? It's not fair. I am older than she is and I am her aunt and raised her and changed her diapers and now the only thing I have is, "Stop talking! You're bothering us!" The only time I have control over Aya is when I go upstairs to study and she follows me because she wants my shoes to build a building and when she wants candy. Strange girl, ha???

But what can I do? I love this little girl more than anything in this life. And I really forget about my nephew who is now six months old. Maybe it's because he is a boy and Aya is a girl and girls are nicer than boys. Or maybe it's because Aya is the first baby to call me Aunt Hadiya. Or maybe it's because he is still too young. But I really love him and enjoy my time with him. When I hug him tightly, he is just like a mouse between my arms. He is really a cute boy. So long.

Your friend,
Hadiya.

OCTOBER 20 CHAT

Hadiya: Today is the last day of Ramadan...

Sasha: So tomorrow when the fast breaks, is this what is called Eid?

Hadiya: Tomorrow is al-Eid and all the family are coming to our house. We will be able to eat all day. About fifty persons will come. I have five uncles and two aunts and they are coming with their children and their grandchildren. Each family will cook one kind of food...

Sasha: Sounds lovely. Do you say 'Happy Eid'?

Hadiya: We say 'Antum Bekar.' It doesn't really mean happy...

OCTOBER 24 CHAT

Hadiya: Yesterday was a really busy day. We had more than forty-five people here and the house was turned upside down. We had to clean and wash dishes but we had fun anyway.

Sasha: Are you eating leftovers from the feast today?

Hadiya: Today we go to visit the relatives. We usually visit my father's cousins every Eid. And my grandfather's cousins. But we still have some relatives to visit tomorrow...

Sasha: Do you eat at each house?

Hadiya: Yes. They usually prepare coffee and some sweets. We have two Eids in the year. One has three days and the other four. The next will come in a few months. It is called Eid al-Adha. In this Eid, the people give the poor people meat.

NOVEMBER 5 CHAT

Hadiya: Hello... After all that happened today, I certainly do not feel good.

Sasha: What happened? Is your family OK?

Hadiya: Didn't you watch the news? The judge decided that Saddam must be killed. I don't know how you say that in English. There is a curfew today so I didn't go to school.

Sasha: Are people angry? Is that why there is a curfew?

Hadiya: Yes all Sunna are angry. Some Shias are happy. Some people just want to cry like me. Some people feel that they will never feel peace in their lives.

Sasha: This sounds like a bad situation...

Hadiya: Do you know what? I didn't love Saddam ever. Now I do. They made me love him ... And the Americans killed more than he did! When we were in Saddam's time, we hardly had any money to eat but we were safe... Now we live in hell.

Sasha: Oh Hadiya, do you think your neighborhood will be safe?

Hadiya: I don't care. The worse thing that can happen is to die. It has become something I want to happen because now my life has no meaning. I don't know where I belong. I don't know who I am or what I want. I don't know anything only that I want to go out of here. I want to escape...

FRIDAY, NOVEMBER 24

Goodbye

Hi all.

With tears and emotion, we have to say goodbye to the people we love even if we don't want to leave each other. We have to say goodbye. Goodbye with no reply.

Hanan, my Christian friend and one of my best friends, I don't know what to say except that I was lucky to have had such a beautiful friend like you. I truly love you from the depths of my heart but I didn't know that I loved you that much. I thought that my friends were all the same and that I didn't love one more than the other. But today, I found out I was wrong.

Hanan was special. She never hurt me or said something to bother me. To better or worse this life will lead us, I don't know which. But I swear by the name of God, I shall never forget you, my sister.

It's this life that makes us suffer and separate. Who was thinking that you would leave me, leave Iraq, leave your past life and everything behind?

I don't know what to say but I know today, I saw my friend for the last time and only God knows if I will ever see her again. She and her family are leaving for Syria for the moment and then they are going to move to Canada. They received a threat and they have to leave Iraq or they will be killed. I know it's better for them to leave but...she is my best friend.

Today we had a party in the garden of my school and it was full of tears. My friends and I were waiting for Hanan to arrive and when she showed up, we all burst into tears. With nothing but tears and hugs, we said hi and bye to her. She gave each one of us one of her toys. It was nice of her to give us some of her personal stuff. I am sure that I will remember that this toy belonged to her.

As my teacher said, our country is losing Hanan. I hope it is that simple because we are all losing, losing everything, even our country. All the people are leaving Iraq. My uncle and my aunts left for Dubai. My other aunt moved from Baghdad to Mosul and by the end of the year, I think we will have my grandparents in our house. Do you know that I haven't seen my grandparents for more than a year?

I think that we are hardly living here, that we hardly keep going in this life. I wish sometimes that my eyes were a digital camera so you could see what I see. Or that you would have a magic ball that would help you to see me and see everything around me. Maybe then you can feel my pain.

Sasha: If you could change the whole world, what would you change?

Hadiya: I would change the people in it...

Sasha: How do you feel your life would be different if the war had not happened?

Hadiya: I believe I was going to be someone different from the girl that I am now. I'm not sure that I would be more special. War has played a part in my life and personality. But not all for the bad.

Sasha: What is the one important thing you would like people to know about you?

Hadiya: I am not a girl who accepts living in silence. Maybe I don't have that much power to change the world but I believe that I have some power to control myself...

Sasha: Was there anything you believed was true as a small child that you later found out was not true?

Hadiya: I believed that human beings got taller as they got older. And my biggest fear was what will we do when my grandparents became older. Would we have to remove the roof?

UNnormal

Time. It is only time that is moving forward. It's the only thing that's doing its job. It's the only thing that we both share. We both live in the same time.

I am still searching for the unknown and hoping that I will find it. But the problem is if I find it, will I know this is what I have been looking for?

Well, I don't know where to start. In fact, I don't want to start talking

about what happened. It's bigger than me to talk about. It's bigger than what you can understand. It's bigger than we can all imagine.

I start my day without power as usual, waking up and studying and then having my breakfast. Until now, it looks like I have a normal life. But hey, did you forget that you are reading IraqiGirl's blog?

Here in this blog, nothing is normal. Here in this blog, people are wearing thick clothes on top of thick clothes until they become like a ball. Many people are drinking dirty water and only

take a bath once a week because the color of the water is closer to black than clear and if you take a bath, you may get dirtier than you are already.

Let's go back to my UNnormal life. One day about a week ago, I was eating my breakfast and took a look through the window to see if the car that takes me to school was waiting there. Yes, there was a car there. No, not a car but an American tank. The road was closed but everything seemed calm.

My parents and my grandma were also having breakfast and I was worrying about my exam that I had that day. I sat on the chair and after that I don't know exactly what happened but there was an explosion near us. The type of explosion that you will always remember. Pieces of the window fell on the floor and the table and in our breakfast. It seemed like it only took a minute and we all ran out of the room. It was a big explosion and plenty of our windows were broken out but we are lucky that our heads were not...

Sasha: Islam is obviously very important to you. Can you talk about why?

Hadiya: In the beginning, I wanted to do everything my parents did. When I learned how to read, I started reading the Quraan. And I started praying when I was nine. And day by day, I have more love for my God and the prophet Muhammad.

Every word I read from the Quraan makes me think of who I am and what I am doing here. When I know there is Allah—someone great who created the mountains, the water, the trees, the earth, and the whole world, how can I ignore him? The water I drink and the food I eat, the ground I walk on, they are all His. If I ignore Allah, I have to leave all the things that He created, leave everything—even my body and my soul. We don't see Allah but we certainly feel him in our hearts. How can I not love the one who created me?

Now I leave you with these words:

When you said the Arabs are all terrorists, that was fine.
But when you destroyed our country and killed our children
and insulted our Prophet
We have to say that is a crime.
I can live with suffering and waiting
Until the next ray of hope shines
But I can't live my life running from you
And agree that Muslims are terrorists
And their hijab is the sign.
I have to tell you that I love the Prophet
And I am proud that his religion
And his God are mine.

The Sajadah (prayer rug) Hadiya prays on

My Future?

MONDAY, JANUARY 1
The end of the end

Am I here because I am someone special? Or am I special because I am someone here?

Because from now on and forever, I want nothing more but only to be here.

I want to be that someone who was born here, was raised here, and dies here.

Am I here living in Iraq or am I imagining myself to be there?

I have a mouth, eyes, and moreover, I have ears. I can hear their whispers. I can see the results of their crimes filling the streets with fear.

The eyes filled with tears...

The hearts filled with fear...

The mouths filled with words,

I wonder if you will ever hear...
Hear their words, their stories.
Hear their tales of this year.
I wonder if you will really dare to hear?

Many things happened that deserve to be written about. But days passed and I thought that I could not write in this blog anymore. I can't say "Happy Eid" for all. I can't say "Happy Christmas" and "Happy New Year" because I would be writing only words that can't do anything for the people who read them.

My words don't leave steps in your hearts. They never will. My words are mine. They only mean something to me because they come from the deepest point in my heart.

You know what? I think I was wrong. My opinions have changed from the first year that I wrote in this blog. I thought then that everything was going to be good and acceptable for all of us—but I was wrong, my friend, I was so wrong.

I was wrong when I said that Saddam didn't mean anything to me. I was wrong when I said I thought he was a bad guy (he still might be but he might not...)

I feel guilty because now I think he is a MAN, a brave man. If you just saw the video that someone took of his execution, you will see no fear from death there. You will see a look in his face of someone who is ready to challenge, someone who believed that he was right. Someone who believed he was doing the right thing after all.

He was smiling. I don't think that I would be smiling if I was in his shoes. I would probably have burst into tears and cried, "Mammeeee!"

Anyway, from now on I'm not going to say anything bad about Saddam because I don't know if he was right or wrong. But I know that the people who came after Saddam are evil and worse than the devil. Saddam was better than them.

And I have to say this: What were they thinking when they executed Saddam on the first day of Eid? Eid is our chance to be happy, to gather with our families and try to forget everything that is bad. And so they turned our happy feelings to sadness. This is the stupidest thing they have done yet. Have these people lost their minds? I am sure of that. Executing Saddam on Eid was a huge mistake, a very huge mistake.

Thank you all for reading this. And a Happy New Year anyway.

Your lost friend from where Iraq once was.

JANUARY 1 CHAT

Hadiya: We haven't had electricity for thirteen hours so we have no heat.

Sasha: How do you heat your house?

Hadiya: We don't. I am wearing a hat right now and I wear layers of clothes—two pairs of trousers and two pairs of socks. It's toooo cold.

Sasha: So did your family do something special for Eid?

Hadiya: All the family gathered in our house to say Eid Mobarak to my grandfather. He is the oldest man in the family and our tradition says that you have to visit him.

Sasha: It must have been special for him and the family that this year, it was possible...

Hadiya: Well, I'm not sure because of his memory. He thought that they came because of the funeral of Saddam. After they left, I asked him if he is happy and he said who can be happy now? I asked him why and he answered who was killed today? And then he said some words about Saddam and his funeral...

Sasha: Dear one. I must eat and then meet a friend. We will go lie in the streets downtown to protest the war...

JANUARY 28 CHAT

Hadiya: There was a big explosion near us today and the road has been closed so my uncle and his son will sleep in our house today and there is a chance that two men we don't know will sleep here too.

Sasha: Who is making these explosions? It must all be so scary and confusing. Are those men safe people? Does your uncle know them well? I hope there is no trouble...

Hadiya: Here is the story. After my uncle (he is the husband of my aunt really) moved to Mosul from their home in Baghdad, they heard that some stranger took up residence in their house, so he went back there and took the things he needed—stuff like the TV—and the cars that carried all their things came to Mosul today. They are moving them into our house.

Sasha: Are things getting worse in Mosul?

Hadiya: The situation in Mosul is very bad but it's worse in Baghdad...

Back to basics

I feel really sorry that I haven't written in a long long time. Well, the first reason was that I was taking my midyear exams and now I have finished them. So I am on my holiday—two weeks of holiday!

This year, our last year of secondary school, we are taking eight basic courses: Physics, Chemistry, Biology, Mathematics, Islam, Arabic, English, French.

In this year, our marks are not important and they don't play a part in going to college. For now, I just need to get more than 50 percent on all my exams. Then I will take the exams that are the most important exams in my life and what grades I get will decide whether I will go to Pharmacy College or Engineering College or any college at all.

I will take those exams in June and till that time the only thing I can do is study, and the only thing you can do for me is pray.

My father is in Syria now. My uncle had a heart attack and needed to have an operation quickly. Three days ago, he had the operation and he is fine, thank God. We are expecting my father to come home today.

The last few weeks were hard for me and harder still for some people who are close to me. Do you remember my friend who had to move to Syria and then she and her family were going to go to Canada? I heard that her father died in Syria a couple of weeks ago. That was horrible. I couldn't stop thinking of her. I was so worried for her. I called her and her voice on the phone was horrible. So please join my prayers for her.

The other horrible news that I heard was that my friend's niece, who is four months younger than Aya, died when she was asleep without any reason. She wasn't sick or anything.

That news made me crazy. Seeing my friend was just as horrible. Whenever she talked to me, we both began to cry. I didn't know what to say to her. I know how much she loved her niece and how hard it is to lose her.

She said some words that made me shiver. She said that when she remembers her niece, she feels as if someone is taking her heart away and now there is nothing in its place. You know, that is exactly what I feel when I think of Baghdad and remember how beautiful it was and how much happier we were in Saddam's time.

If losing a niece hurt her as much as losing a country, then we have to do something for this girl. Because I know what happened to her is bigger than she could bear, bigger than she could believe.

FROM KYLIE:

Dear Hadiya,

I'm sorry about your situation, thanks for telling us what's happening over there.

Now I'm curious about Iraq (I have been reading more about Iraq, how it is a country with a very rich history). Can I ask you how it is over there?

Are you close to Kurdistan? Is it really nice in Kurdistan? And can Sunnis marry Shiites? Can an Iraqi marry a Westerner (like an American)? Or do Iraqis only marry Iraqis? And do boys go to school with girls?

FROM HADIYA:

Dear Kylie,
Well, Mosul is not too close to Kurdistan. You need one and a half hours to reach Kurdistan. Kurdistan is so beautiful; you can find some pictures of Kurdistan if you search in my blog.

In Iraq Sunnis can marry Shia. As a matter of fact two of my relatives married Shias. And Iraqis can marry Westerners. In the primary school, boys and girls go to the same school. But in secondary school, girls and boys each have their own schools. Then they go back together for college.

FEBRUARY 18 CHAT

Hadiya: Remember, I told you we have a lot of books in Baghdad? We want to give them to the library there.

Sasha: Do you know that in the U.S., because they spend so much of our taxes on war, there is no money for public libraries in some places and they are closing down?

Hadiya: No one uses the public library here now. We want to give them to the library in Baghdad, but then when will we be able to go there?

Sasha: How is your grandfather doing?

Hadiya: Yesterday, he was very sick. We were so afraid but today he is better. Yes, I think he is better.

Sasha: How is medical care in Mosul? Are the hospitals OK? Do they have medicines and equipment? Do people get free medical care or do they have to pay?

Hadiya: My father says that the public hospital is free but you can't call it a hospital.

Sasha: Why?

Hadiya: You know what, Sasha? We are in Iraq. The hospitals are dirty. There is no medicine, no care...

Sasha: We are working on getting these things to hospitals in Iraq so please if you can, find out what the hospital needs.

Hadiya: ALL the hospitals need EVERYTHING—except patients...

Sasha: I hate this war—I know you hate it more...

Hadiya: Do you know? I am ready to kill your president if I ever meet him because he killed me, he killed every person in Iraq. He has destroyed our good feelings; he has made our life black.

SATURDAY, MARCH 3

Where we were

I was talking with my mother in the kitchen while she was washing the dishes.

My dad was sitting in the living room watching the news.

They were passing by our house. They were three women and a kid walking in the street. And BOOOOOM!

That's what we heard. My mom jumped from her place. My dad,

as usual, did what he always does when we hear an explosion. He went out of the house. Then there was shooting so I rushed out of the house and pleaded with him to come inside.

When he came inside he was followed by the three women and the child. They were walking in the street and the explosion made them crazy so they ran into our house. They sat for a while and left when the shooting stopped.

The situation is always getting worse. Yesterday, we heard two big explosions every hour. We didn't even fix the kitchen windows that were broken in December because every day we hear another explosion that is big enough to break them out again.

My aunt came from Baghdad a couple of days ago to see my uncle after his operation. The day after she got here, there was a big explosion near the house she was visiting. All the windows were broken and some of the doors. My aunt injured her forehead, but it is small, so don't worry about that.

Two days ago, I went with my friend to visit Mosul University. Our journey was beautiful. We visited my sister's Medicine College and Pharmacy College and some others. The whole university looked so nice, especially my sister's college. But the Pharmacy College looked awful. It was like a jail.

Part of me felt happy after that journey because in no time at all, I will be there in the university. But on the other hand, part of me felt bad because I don't think I belong in the Pharmacy College. Maybe because it's bad looking. Or maybe because my uncle advised me to rethink it. I really don't know but I think I'm beginning to like Architect College.

Your friend,
Hadiya

March 7 Message to Sasha

Well, I have only five minutes to talk. I was reading the Harry Potter story where they talked about a very strong devil wizard, and it made me think...

Some U.S. people, like you Sasha, didn't play a part in making this horrible thing in Iraq. But some did. I don't want to show disrespect or something. I do respect the American people. I just want to change old you-know-who...

April 1 Chat

Hadiya: I am OK. Don't worry.

Sasha: Hello. I've been worried about you. It sounds like things are getting worse in Mosul.

Hadiya: Oh, today was so bad. The window in my father's room was broken out. It was such a bad day, full of big explosions.

Sasha: Who is fighting? Is the U.S. military fighting? You must be terrified...

Hadiya: No. Not really. The only thing that scares me at the moment are the exams.

Sasha: Heh! You are so brave until it comes to your exams.

Hadiya: Have you ever studied these English sounds like "au" and "j" and the others? They kill me. I can't recognize one from the other. This "oo" in pool and foot, is it like the "u" sound? I become so weak during the exams and everything associated with the exams...

Sasha: I am soooo glad you are OK.

Hadiya: Am I?

Sasha: OK. As in being alive.

Hadiya: Yes, I forgot. I am alive if alive means to breathe.

Sasha: Don't let the English language defeat you. You are stronger than it...

WEDNESDAY, AUGUST 8

Hero

I know you missed me and worried about me. Well, you should. I also know I haven't written anything for long long months. So I have many things to talk about and I don't know where to start.

On the first of April, we stopped going to school in order to study for the exams we were supposed to take on June 12th. The first month of studying was excellent. I was studying hard and doing my best.

Did I write that my grandfather and grandmother came from Baghdad to stay with us after my uncle and his wife were forced to leave that city to find what you call a life? The situation became UNbelievable in Baghdad and it was IMpossible for human beings to live there.

In May, my grandfather's health began to get worse day after day. Some mornings I woke up and sat down to breakfast with my mom and she was so close to crying.

I knew that my grandfather was not OK that morning. I entered his room and said hello and he opened his mouth but he couldn't reply. But I knew...that he heard me.

I don't know what I was thinking. I went to my room to study. I was trying to persuade myself that my grandfather would be fine and it was just the same as usual. But I really knew he was not and that his day was today.

Anyway, I lost my grandfather that day while I was studying upstairs. He was more than my grandfather. He was my hero and always will be.

MONDAY, AUGUST 20

The smell of knowledge

It was a time when men were real men and women real women and their innocent little children were the hope of change and a better future.

It was a time when the Iraqi people were like a big family. A time where friends were brothers and brothers real friends.

It was a time when life was simple and people lived a simple life.

In 1921, my grandpa was born in Mosul, Iraq on February 5th. He was the youngest child among his brothers and sisters.

My grandfather grew up in the middle of a big family. Unfortunately, he lost his mother when he was a little child, and that affected him greatly. Until his last days, he was always mentioning his mom and he missed her impressively.

His brothers didn't finish their secondary school. But despite that, we can't say anything but that they were really educated and that a book was always in their hands.

In that time, the number of people who were able to finish high school was very small. So his two brothers went to learn how to practice their family vocation that was passed down through the generations. Everyone admired their kind of work and their reputation passed from father to son.

Unlike his brothers, my grandfather continued his studies and he was so eloquent that he graduated from high school and went on to college.

In 1943, he finished studying to be a civil engineer at the American University in Beirut.

In 1959, he earned his post-graduate diploma in hydraulic engineering in Holland.

Then, in 1962, he was awarded a Ph.D. in irrigation and drainage engineering at Utah State University in the USA.

After that, he returned to Iraq and occupied many important positions. He was even appointed vice president in charge of establishing a university in Mosul, in addition to being dean of his college at the new university. He had many similar positions later in Baghdad. He was also a member of scientific academies all over the world.

He composed six books in his lifetime. When he retired in 1986, he was nominated Professor Emeritus of Irrigation at the University of Baghdad.

I am so proud to be a granddaughter of such a person and I dream of the day when I will go back to sleep and say to myself, "If my grandfather were here, he would be proud of me."

As a granddaughter, I had grown up away from my grandpa, as he was living in Baghdad and I was living in Mosul.

When I was a little child, my grandfather was that man with glasses who was always reading books. He was also the first person in our family to have a computer. The first computer—the only one I had seen until I was the age of six—was my grandfather's computer.

When I became a teenager, I began to see how respected my grandfather was. When people said that I was clever, they would comment, "just like her grandpa." When I go to the university with my mom, old men come and say, "I was your grandfather's student."

When we used to go to Baghdad to spend the holiday there, my grandfather was an inspiration to me. By then all the family members had-computers—but we didn't have his amazing room, which was always filled with books, hundreds and hundreds of them.

That room made me feel like I was in a library. I remember when I was a little kid, how much I loved to be in that room. I was always looking for an opportunity to sneak in there.

When I was ordered to call my grandfather for lunch, it was an order that I obeyed with pleasure. Now I imagine myself in a cartoon movie. I have red hair and am dressed in cartoon clothes and I sneak into my grandfather's room and stop in the middle of all the books and I am examining the titles and then my grandfather catches me there. It's a funny dream but it never happened. And I don't have red hair anyway.

What I noticed in that room was the smell, the same smell that my grandpa had, a nice and weird smell... the smell of knowledge.

Nice days...nice memories—and painful ones. Now that room and the big house in Baghdad is empty of people. It hurts me that we can't go to that house because it is in Baghdad.

When I buy a book, I think of one thing: Did my grandfather have this book? Many precious books that I want to read are there in that room far away from my hands.

Here in Mosul is where my grandfather died. I am happy that he returned to his place of birth and died where he wanted to die and was buried as he wished, between his brother and his father.

All I want to say is, "I love you, my grandpa..."

August 29 Chat

Hadiya: Hey...

Sasha: Hey back. How are you?

Hadiya: I am angry with myself. I feel like I am an evil person. I was talking with my friend who was going to go to Medicine College. I just wanted to advise her not to make the stupidest decision of her life so I told her why I didn't want to be a doctor and what my sister suffered in Medicine College.

She suddenly lost her smile and said she hadn't thought of all those problems but that she would now. And then she disappeared and I am feeling like a person who killed someone's dream. I am evil...

Sasha: We do these things sometimes, thoughtless things...

Hadiya: I am not sure of my dream but she was sure of hers... I am crying now. I want my grandpa... I want to die but I am afraid of dying. That is a bad place to be in. Heaven will never be a bad place but I want to make sure where I will be.

I wish I lived in Mohammad's time when Islam was still new... I wish I could see Mohammad. I wonder how he looked.

Sasha: He probably looked like any man. Maybe if he walked by you on the street in Mosul today, you would not think he was anyone special...

Hadiya: Sometimes I feel jealous of people who love Mohammad more than I do.

Sasha: How do you know they love him more than you?

Hadiya: Because when they talk about Mohammad they cry. I only cry sometimes when I read the Quraan...

FRIDAY, SEPTEMBER 8
Life is difficult...

On June 11th, only one day separated us from the first day of our examinations.

I woke up in the morning with a smile on my face because finally I was going to take these exams after all that studying and studying. I had breakfast with my father and I remember very well that he told me, "the exams will never end if you don't start them."

By noon, there were only fifteen hours left before the exams started. My mobile rang and there was one new message. It was from my cousin and he said that the exams had been postponed.

I didn't believe that. I thought he was joking and playing with me. How could they postpone the exams??

But it wasn't a game. All Iraqi students in their last year of high school should have been taking their Islam exam tomorrow.

To believe or not to believe was not our choice because it really did happen and the exam was really postponed until the first of July. News came to us that the questions were leaked and they had to change them.

So it was really a game.

I rushed upstairs and took a bath and tried to feel better. After a couple of hours, I began to study Arabic because I had an Arabic examination the day after tomorrow.

The next morning, the smile came back to my face. I finished my studying before breakfast and when I sat down at the table I told my family that I was a little scared and only ate a few bites before my mother's mobile rang. She went to the next room to talk to someone and then came back to the kitchen with a rather long face.

When I saw her, my heart began to throb hard and then she said, "Hadiya..." and I said, "No, no, not again" and she said, "yes" and I crashed into tears. I cried so hard that all the family around the table were feeling so sorry at how bad I looked because my examination was postponed again. My sister was really worried and kept asking my father to do something for me. So my father gave me a Valium and I went up to bed and cried for a long time. In the morning, I looked at myself in the mirror and my eyes were swollen and looked red.

The postponement was because there was a curfew in Baghdad!
Anyway, that too has passed.
To be continued.

TUESDAY, SEPTEMBER 11

...Life is hard

Another morning and another day. I woke up and said to myself for the third time that week, "Tomorrow, I will start my examinations..."
Scared? Yes. I was so scared that they would postpone the exam again. I was feeling uncomfortable and unsettled.

I heard on the news that there was a curfew in Basra and I expected that they would postpone my Arabic exam so I didn't start studying until 4 p.m. when I was able to overcome my disappointment.

Finally, a new day came. A very precious and wanted day. The day of our first examination!

I was nervous in the morning before I went to my school. I still couldn't believe that I would really take the exam. Until the last second before it started, I was confident the Ministry of Education would announce another surprise.

Anyway, I finally took the Arabic exam and I did well. The other examinations passed smoothly and by the third of July, I was finished.

I was so happy to be in the holiday, the holiday that I had been waiting for so long, but it was sad that I had to miss my cousin's engagement. Still, I reached one of the hardest accomplishments in my life. I finished high school. I am from now on, a fresh woman.

A few weeks after the exams were finished, we went to Syria to see my uncle and aunt—they left Iraq in 2004 and we had not seen them since then. So it was nice to visit with them and my new cousin.

We spent good and happy times in Syria and after fifteen days of a quiet, peaceful life we returned to our home. We were so sad and so glad to return to Iraq.

But on our way back to Iraq, we had a little accident. The driver was making a call on his mobile while he was driving the car and a child was standing in the middle of the road and the driver didn't see him.

My uncle was sitting next to the driver. He was half asleep but he saw the child and yelled, "Look ahead!" That's what I heard before the car went right and left and left and right and then the car knocked something and kept running straight ahead very UNstraightly. After a minute that felt like an hour, it finally came to a stop and we were all in shock, looking at each other with our full, open eyes. Thank Allah, the child was still alive so we took him with us in the car to the nearest hospital. We had to change cars there because the driver stayed with the boy in the hospital.

The car that transported us to Iraq was so old. It had no air conditioning so we were dying for ten hours. The accident must have been a message from our country. After about a week (just joking), we reached our house.

A week ago, I received my marks. They were good marks but not the ones I was expecting nor the marks I deserved—but they were still good. My average was 94.4 but I got special points for taking French, which made my average 97.6.

These marks will enable me to go to any college I want.

So what college am I planning to go to? That's what you'll know in the next post.

SEPTEMBER 17 CHAT

Sasha: How are you?

Hadiya: We are OK. Today there was a car bomb very close to our house. It really didn't make a loud sound. The police knew about it before it exploded and they announced there is a car bomb and we opened all the windows so they wouldn't break out.

Sasha: Have things changed? Is it more or less dangerous for you to go out than it was a year ago? Or the same?

Hadiya: No, not the same. It's more dangerous now.

TUESDAY, SEPTEMBER 25
Scattered words

Hundreds and hundreds of miles separated us from the edge.
Plans, dreams, and success were the fences of our age.
Days came and passed away. We were at the top of the stage.
But sorry to tell you, my friend, now my heart is full of rage.

WEDNESDAY, SEPTEMBER 26
Sudden hope

Hope came yesterday and I don't know why it came.
Did it come to say goodbye? Or did it come to say that it was satisfied?

THURSDAY SEPT. 27
Hidden tears

I admit and acknowledge that my dreams are dreams.
And my ambition is ambition.
And my destiny is a destiny.
And my faith is my faith.

And my soul is a soul.
But what I cannot admit and cannot understand
Is why is my life not my own?
I feel like someone being led
Like someone being controlled.
Like someone stifling her voice and hiding her tears
Who keeps pretending to be fine
And wishes that she really was.

THURSDAY OCTOBER 4

Excuses

"Remember, remember the first of October/
the gunpowder, treason, and plot/I see no reason why the
gunpowder and treason/should ever be forgot..."
"Remember, remember the first of October/
the date of disaster/the date of..."

ANOTHER DISASTER!

The first of October was the first day of university after the summer holidays. Najma, my sister, was so eager to start her second year of college. What can I say? She is so weird!

My sister and my mother went to Mosul University. If my sister's lessons ended early, they planned that she should come to my mother's college and they would return home together. If not, Najma should wait near her college for my dad.

Although Najma is not a good listening girl, she followed the instructions perfectly.

About 1 p.m., a car bomb exploded where Najma and my dad had agreed to meet. I was in the house counting the walls in each room and guess what? There are four walls in each room, not more, not less.

I didn't hear the explosion but I heard my cell phone ringing. It was my dad calling me.

Alo, where are you?

Dad, this is Hadiya. Is there any place I could be except home?

I thought I called your mother. Hang up the phone!

OK, OK, but it's not my fault, is it?

What I thought was that my mother hadn't met my dad in the usual place they planned to meet (as usual). But the truth was that my father was calling my mother because he saw a car bomb and a fire where he was supposed to meet Najma so he called my mother to see if my sister had arrived at her college and survived.

Did she die or did she not? That is the question.

Well, yes, she finished her lessons early and went to my mother's college. There is where she heard the car bomb's explosion. There is where my mother sat shocked because she was so close to losing a daughter. And there is where Najma found a new reason not to do housework.

"I was going to die today and you want me to wash the dishes?"

So they met my dad and they ran back home before the police closed off the street.

And later, while I was studying the theory that says, "all rooms have but one ceiling," my cell phone rang again. It was my mom and she said, "We are going to see your cousin. A car bombing took place near the university and he was injured."

Suddenly, without any warning, my tears fell and I asked in a shaking voice, "How is he?" My mother assured me that he was OK. But they hadn't seen him yet. He had driven his own car home and gone to his house.

Later, my cousin told them the whole story. He was shopping in front of the university, buying watermelon, when a car in the next street exploded. The sound was so loud that my cousin couldn't believe he could still hear.

After the explosion, he said he found himself lying on the ground far away from where he had been standing. He said there was money and watermelons everywhere. His clothes had been torn and he had injuries in his legs.

The situation was very confusing. There were six injured people (four of them were students) and one dead man (a teacher in the university). This is the information I heard on the news. But of course there were more injured people that were not counted—the news cannot cover everything.

My cousin left that place and drove his car to his house before his mother and wife heard the news. He left his money and the watermelon he bought on the ground as a sign. The sign says:

Here is where a man was lying...

Here is where a man left his belongings

And took his soul to his child and family,

A soul, which is maybe a reason of the life of this man.

In the end, I couldn't improve on the theory that, "the room has but one ceiling."

TUESDAY, OCTOBER 9

Truth will prevail

First I have an announcement. If you would like to visit my house, you are welcome. You can find me in there anytime. I am not going anywhere. I don't intend to go anywhere. I would be lying if I said I don't like to go outside and visit with people but I can't because there is a curfew and it is Ramadan. You are a very dear guest.

So I am spending my holiday in my house. Don't think it's a boring holiday. I am doing the sort of things you do on holiday. Some-times I go for a walk, taking steps from one room to another. From the kitchen to the guest room, from the bathroom to the bedroom. And sometimes I make progress and go into our backyard just for a walk in the garden. You know, walking is a good sport...

It seems like the pilots of the American airplanes heard about my interest in the sound of their warplanes (not true). They really seem like they have an order not to let anyone sleep.

I am sorry for disappointing them. I woke up one morning and I found myself in love with the sound they make. It's not like other sounds. These sounds are special and sound natural. They are like the song in my head. They are not merely an annoying, ugly, awful hideous sound, an impossible sound. These sounds help mothers to hush their babies. They help the community to discover the value of silence.

"If speech is made from silver, than silence is spun from gold..."

I am not a bookish girl. I never will be. But the bad situation in Mosul gave me an unexpected present. It's a space-time thing. I find myself reading one book after another. I put down one book and begin reading another. I don't know why I didn't do this ages ago. Reading is really amusing and a useful habit. I read a police story written by Agatha Christie. And I read two books in the Harry Potter series and some other stories. Reading a book is much easier than writing a book, don't you think?

I am still holding tightly to what hope I have remaining, especially after I survived last night.

At about 1 a.m., I went out of my room. I was half asleep and my eyes were nearly closed but I saw a creature with green evil eyes look-ing at me. It acted like it had an invitation to enter my room. It was walking toward me when my brain finally received a call that this creature is a CAT!

"CAAAAAAAAAAT!" I shouted loudly and ran back to my room and closed the door behind me before it could get in. I begin to yell and scream for help. "There is a cat in the house!" I shouted and Najma (my sister who knows very well how much I hate cats and how much I am afraid of even the sight of them) woke up my father and told him the story.

My father came upstairs to my room and he saw the cat running out the window. He told me that the cat had left and that I was safe now. But I insisted that he walk downstairs with me hand in hand. My father was very furious with me and said, "You are lucky that the cat didn't eat you."

I didn't expect him to be proud of my brave behavior. I was really shaking and full of fear. Anyway, I survived—and the cat didn't eat me.

Najma, as usual, didn't stop giggling at me. Hmm, I miss the old times when I was the brave girl and she didn't have the courage to come into the kitchen alone. You see, I invented the story that there was a ghost named Shrurah living in there, and after that she wouldn't enter the kitchen without being accompanied.

I don't know why the people here are bored and always wishing they could leave Iraq. Najma, for example, is reading a book called *Faster Than the Speed of Light*. It is about transport across time (I told you she is weird but you didn't listen!) Najma wants to live in the future without living in the present. Yuk!

Why would anybody want to live in the future since everything is only going to get worse? Why does anybody want to live another second, another hour, another day, anyway?

Who said that Najma will find herself in the future? Who said that she will be alive? Who said there will be a life? It's very difficult to understand the incentives that make her think there will be a better future.

Your friend from the present,

Hadiya (the Survivor).

Sasha: I read about your cousin being hurt in the blog. How is he?

Hadiya: He's good. I told you not to worry. But Najma hasn't gone to the university since the day she was almost killed. My mom and dad won't let her go. But who says our house is any safer?

Sasha: I wanted to tell you that I will mail your package from Amman. I will be there at the end of the month.

Hadiya: O.k. but promise me that it is the last present you will send me. You don't have to send me a present. Well, maybe a book.

FRIDAY, OCTOBER 19

Just talking

On the 11th of October, the sound of a huge explosion woke me up from my dear sleep. A bomb in a van exploded in the neighborhood near al-Sina'a. Many people died and many people lost their stores and other buildings.

I feel sorry for those who lost their stores and their buildings (I have a heart, you know) but am I really sorry for the people who died? I don't think so (see, I really don't have a heart). I feel sorry for their parents and their children but I don't really feel sorry for them. Life is not what we are good at. I am not sorry because I know they were not happy.

Life is a game and it's so clear that we are losing it. The people who died are obviously the people who pressed "quit" to end the game. It's maybe unwise to end the game before we finish it—but they win the battle even if they don't win the war.

If you are away from violence, life can go on and on (a drowning man will clutch at a straw).

Since we came back from Syria, Najma and I have spent hours and hours every day trying on our new clothes. But one question kept repeating itself: When will we really be able to wear them?

Finally the first day of Eid has come and I was able to put on my new clothes. (I wondered why they looked so familiar in the pictures we took.)

On the first day of Eid, all my uncles, aunts, and cousins came to our house. It is the first Eid after my grandpa's death and it's a tradition to visit the family of the dead person during al-Eid.

My father's cousin also came to the house. All I did all day on the first day of Eid was boil water and make and serve the coffee. After seven hours of making and serving coffee, I was completely tired but really happy indeed.

Here are some photos of what we ate for Eid.

Now Ramadan and Eid are over and our usual boring lives remain and are not over.

Do you know what else is over? This post is over.

Or not

Are we crazy or are we not?

A couple of days ago, Najma's friend said she was coming to our house the next day. Najma was planning to make a sweet for her but she didn't have time to make it during the day. About 1 a.m., while I was working on the computer, I saw a light in the kitchen. My sister had surely lost her mind cooking sweets after midnight, I thought.

A minute later, she came and asked me to help her, which is something I am always ready to do, especially if it's cooking. So there we were both in the kitchen cooking and laughing and trying not to make noise so we wouldn't be caught by my grandma or my mom who would definitely tell everyone that we were up all night cooking sweets. My aunt-in-law would spread the word and we would be the major subject in the latest gossip. Meanwhile, we were enjoying ourselves and wondering if we were crazy or not.

In the middle of all this, the electricity went off.

So now we were cooking in the dark and laughing and we were sure that we were crazy. The dark didn't stop us from making the sweets. Thank Allah that we didn't get caught but there certainly must have been a shocked look on my mother's face when she opened the refrigerator the next morning and saw our sweets.

Is there a curfew or is there not?

The next day, Najma's friend came to our house but she only stayed for a quarter of an hour because her brother called and said a policeman had told him that there was a curfew. Minutes later, her father came to take her home and she went without even tasting the sweets that we were up all night cooking.

An hour later, the curfew ended.

Are we chickens or are we not?

One fact is that there are no cars in the street after 7 p.m. Another fact says that Iraqi people go to sleep around 10 p.m. The question is when do chickens go to sleep, before or after 10 p.m.?

In my case and in Najma's case and in the case of every young Iraqi, we won't go to bed before 11 p.m. because we are... I don't know. But in our parents' case, oh yeah, they do go to bed early. My mom was talking with her brother in the United Arab Emirates on the computer and he said it was only 9 p.m. and he was going out to eat ice cream. Mom told him that she was fighting to stay awake until 10 p.m. He didn't believe that and asked her, "Are you chickens?"

So really, are we chickens?

Is this a life or is this not?

I can't forget that during Saddam's time, we went out to eat ice cream every night after midnight. Oh, I want the old days to come back. I want to see the moon and the sky in the afternoon. I want to see that hope is coming soon. I want to see life like a movie cartoon and not like a scary movie night.

I want to be a normal girl living a normal life. Not this girl who is sitting in front of the computer, writing a diary and trying to be such a funny, lovely girl. I want to take off Hadiya's nickname and I want to throw out all her bad memories and I want to clean her heart of pain. And I want just to be myself and just to talk for myself and just to hear my voice and just to be who I am.

I just want to be...

To be someone else.

P.S. I wonder if it is me who wrote this blog or was it she? Or not?

Yours,

Me, Myself, *not* I

You've got someone to share cooking with at late night — very nice, stick to her as much as possible; I don't eat at night frequently as I have to eat on my own, without anyone else.

FROM HADIYA:

I will follow your advice and stick around Najma :) Weird how our relationship changed in the last year. She was my enemy, not my sister, and now she is my friend more than my sister.
We grow up, I guess.

FRIDAY, NOVEMBER 2

Dreams and decisions

Salaam to all.

As you know, I finished high school with a good average, high enough to enter any college I want. After I got my grades, I began to think seriously about what I wanted to be. I always dreamed of going to Pharmacy College, but for some reason, I hesitated about putting it down as my first option. To be a pharmacist is a good and suitable job for me if I work in Iraq. But will I have a future as a pharmacist if I have to leave Iraq? I don't trust that the situation here will be better tomorrow.

So I was between choosing to go to Pharmacy College, Dentistry College, or Arts Cultural College. I asked for advice. People gave me their opinions and I was completely lost. I was really unable to make a decision and that made me feel very frustrated.

After a while, I removed Arts Cultural College from my list. I began to change my mind every day. Every day, I made a different decision and every day, I fell apart.

Finally, I made a comparison between the College of Dentistry and the College of Pharmacy and these are the conclusions this led me to:

If I choose Dentistry College, I will be called a doctor. I will have a job in the future outside Iraq. Dentistry College is easier to study for than Pharmacy College. The Dentistry College building looks great. But, on the other hand, I will be hated by all children—and I'm not sure that I won't hate myself too. I can't imagine putting my hand in someone's mouth. I can't stand the smell of mouths. In the end, I asked my dentist for advice and he said that pharmacy is more suitable for women.

But pharmacy is a very hard college. I may not have a good future with a job. The Pharmacy College building looks like a jail. On the other hand, pharmacists are called chemists in some countries and I very much like chemistry and am in love with everything associated with it. Pharmacy College was always the college I dreamed of.

So I took my pen and wrote: "Mosul University, the College of Pharmacy" as the first choice and "Mosul University, the College of Dentistry" as my second choice.

Usually, the College of Medicine is the number one choice. You need to have the highest grades... Although my marks were high enough to go to Medicine College, I never wanted to be a doctor. It's a hard job in Iraq, especially after the war. Doctors are in danger of being kidnapped and murdered, plus they have to sleep in the hospitals. And I am completely surrounded by doctors—my father, my uncle, my big sister, and my brother-in-law are all doctors. I don't think I would be good at being a doctor, seeing blood, seeing injured people. I have a weak heart. I know I couldn't stand seeing all that.

Anyway, I chose Pharmacy College, but I still have to take an exam and my grade will lead me to one of two Colleges, either Pharmacy or Dentistry.

I am eager to go to college but the problem is that I'm not studying. I can't focus on what I am reading. I read the book and my mind is somewhere else. I try and try but I get nothing. I can't help it. But my grades are still high and my position still is good even if I get zero on the exam.

See you later,
The Girl Who Was Hadiya

TUESDAY, NOVEMBER 13

Eyes on my life

The winter is coming on and the weather gets colder every day. Najma and Aya already have the flu and I haven't been feeling so fine myself the last couple of days.

I have very good news. I was accepted in the Pharmacy College at Mosul University. I am so eager to start a new life as a college student and go through this experience. I still remember very well my first steps in the primary school and how scared I was to go there. And how I spent my first days there following Najma from place to place. Najma, poor girl, is happy because I didn't apply to her college. Who wants to have a sister in the same college anyway?

It is a great opportunity for me to get away from her eyes and just be me. But my cousin who is two years older than me is also studying pharmacy in the same college so I can't really do my stupidities and get away from my relatives without being noticed. I know that my cousin is a very good boy and he will help me but I'm not really relieved to have a relative in my college.

I am still not sure when I will start Pharmacy College but I guess the time is not far away. I am very excited. I will see people. I will walk in the streets. I will have a life.

One little problem that is coming: all our courses are in English. I know my English is good but I don't know any of the medical words. I can't even pronounce most of them. I am searching for a medical dictionary. It would be better if it was English-Arabic. If you find a dictionary for me, I can download it on the computer...

The situation in Mosul is still getting worse, although some things are better. A few roads, which have been closed for the last two months, were opened today.

Speaking of negative situations, our neighbor's brother who was about thirty years old, married with a kid, didn't return home one day. They thought that he had been kidnapped and they waited for a call from the people who had kidnapped him so they could pay the money for his release. Unfortunately, no one ever called. And two days later, he was found in the post-mortem room. Today our neighbor called and said he is leaving for Armenia.

The basic fact is that we are still insecure and in danger even when we are in our own homes. But life goes on.

Your pharmacist friend from Iraq

SATURDAY, DECEMBER 1

Me and my new life

I am on my way to the future and living what possibly could be a happy memory someday.

I started college six days ago and it's...it's...

It's a life beyond my normal life. Something wonderful, something new. It's what I need.

We are taking seven subjects. They are Physiology, Cell Biology, Organic Chemistry, English, Medical Statistics, Anatomy, and Human

Rights. All are in English except for Human Rights.

Physiology looks interesting especially because Dr. Basaam is a wonderful man. He really works hard. I have had great respect for him since the first lesson.

Next week, we will have our first physiology lab and Dr. Basaam

asked each student to bring a frog with them. I have an idea about what we will do to those frogs but you really don't want to know. The problem is that I can't find any frogs in our garden. I asked all of my relatives to look in their gardens for one for me but I don't have any frog yet. In spite of the fact that I love frogs, I am so eager to.... "you know."

Dr. Omar who teaches anatomy, seems good too. He is a popular teacher in both the Pharmacy and Medicine Colleges.

Cell biology or Cytology is being taught by Dr. Farah, who is a woman. She is good too, but she talks so fast and gives us so much homework.

Medical Statistics is my biggest nightmare. I don't like it. But I studied the lesson one more time with my mom and I think I understand it now. Inshallah.

We are about 120 students in Pharmacy College. The boys are not more than twenty-five. They are so polite and quiet and studying all the time. When we have our rest time, the girls spread out in the university and we go to buy sandwiches and have fun and the boys stay in their places like old men who have nothing to do but read books. They make me angry. Why all that studying?

The most enjoyable class I had this week was the Human Rights lesson. The teacher asked us to define what human rights are and the boys spoke up for the first time ever. One boy commented that not all people deserved to be called humans. This made everyone laugh. I don't know why all the boys and girls couldn't control themselves. One other boy began talking about the French Revolution. He said that he had read a book about it just to make sure everyone knew that he had once read a book. He talked about this revolution as an answer to every question but his answers didn't make any sense.

During this month, I thought a lot about me and who I really am: And I decided that I need a lot more time to spend with me so I will work hard this year for me. Me is the one that I really don't know. I don't know what color she likes. What desserts she loves. Which stories are her favorites? And who she is really?

She, maybe the girl that survives...
The one that will always be alive...
Maybe the victim of this war...
Maybe the one you are looking for...
Maybe it's the rain that's falling down...
Maybe the one who never wants to be down...
Maybe the weakest girl in the world...
But not the weakest letter in these words...

For the sake of me and my dreams, for the sake of the smile that was given to no one but me, for the sake of my grandpa and for the sake of my country and for the sake of my religion and for the sake of my God, I will be a better person this year. I will find me.

I will not give up trying to do something to change the bad situation around me. I want to know my destination. I want to draw the whole road that opens before me. And in the end, maybe life will be secure.

2008–2009
My Present
Interview by Elizabeth Wrigley-Field

What made you decide to start your blog? You chose to blog in English—why? Were you trying to reach Americans?

When my sister Najma started blogging, I thought, She's no better than me! If she can do it, I can blog too.

But in the beginning, I really had problems with blogging, because my English wasn't good enough to write a whole sentence... so what about a whole blog post?! My father used to help me by correcting my spelling and grammar. With time, I found myself more able to express my feelings in English—maybe even more so than in Arabic.

I chose to blog in English because:

1. I wanted to improve my English language abilities

2. Most of the visitors to my blog are foreign, not Iraqi, and most are English speakers

3. Iraqi and Arab people are already aware of what's going on in Iraq, much more than Europeans and American people. Your news channels don't cover everything, and in fact they sometimes show things not as they are, but as they want them to be. They change the facts, when the truth should prevail.

I had an Arabic blog, but I haven't posted on it in ages! And I used to write a diary on a small copybook, starting when I was twelve years old. I would write down everything I held inside, which was a big relief.

What have you liked best about blogging?

The benefits I've gotten from blogging are:

1. I became more satisfied about what I am doing during the war. At least I feel that I am doing something, even if it's just writing.

2. I've made friends from other countries who are writing to me, worrying about me. It lets me feel that there are people watching over me. [People s]uch as Sasha Crow and John Ross, who both worked hard to get this book published. I owe them so much, for the confidence they have in me.

What are you doing nowadays? What's your experience as a college student been like?

I am a human studying machine these days rather than a human being. I do nothing but study, which makes me feel pretty isolated from what is happening around me. Sometimes I look in the mirror and say, "Wow, who is she, and why is she staring at me?"

But this was an unusual year for me as a student, because on some days I couldn't study. Not for any specific reason, I just felt tired of working. Listening to the news without being able to do anything, doing nothing but eating, it made me feel useless.

There's an Egyptian poet named Ahmad Matar, who wrote lines something like this (my imperfect translation):

An ant protected by me
lying under my feet
peacefully living for years
since my last leg movement

Sometimes that's what I feel like. Years since my last leg movement. But not all the time.

Life as a college student is so different from life in high school. All Iraqi schools are either for boys or for girls, but in college there are no limits. In college we deal with mature people, who often have dreams and determination to change the whole circumstances around us for the better. People demonstrate, they march, they do philanthropic work like visiting orphans' houses and collecting money for them, and many other great things. These all let me feel that there's hope for people.

What do you plan to do when you finish college?

Really good question. Well, when I entered college I thought I would be first in my class and I would continue on my road to being a lecturer at Pharmacy College. I love teaching. But my marks aren't high enough to let me follow that dream, so I will either open a pharmacy, or if I have the opportunity, continue studying.

You're now nineteen years old. What do you think looking back on what you wrote when you were fifteen, sixteen years old?

I think I had the worst English ever, and I don't know why people paid any attention to what I wrote when the sentences were not even understandable. Maybe they had a joyous time laughing at me.

How do you look back on the war and its effect on your life today?

I think war is the worst thing that can ever happen to any country. It is a disaster.

It affected my life so strongly; for one thing, now I'm growing up with no grandparents. My grandparents from my father's side died before I was six, but my grandparents from my mother's side were living in Baghdad. I was always so jealous of my friends who went to their grandparents' house every Friday, but we went to Baghdad for every summer holiday besides Eid. The days I spent in Baghdad were the happiest days of the year for me. I had family all around me, since my grandparents, aunts, and uncles all lived in the same neighborhood.

After the war, everything changed. The situation in Baghdad (like in other cities, too) became so bad that my uncle Ahmed left Iraq. After that, the trip to Baghdad wasn't so fun. I had never seen my grandma crying before, but after he left I did. It's hard to lose a son. My grandpa, who loved Ahmed's daughter more than everything else in life, was really suffering after they left. His sadness began affecting his health, and about a year after Ahmed left, my aunt left Iraq too. My other uncle, who had had successful work in Baghdad, had no option but to leave too. My grandparents moved into our house in Mosul before he left.

Now the family has five empty houses in Baghdad. Now I have no family there except my mother's cousins.

After my grandparents settled in our house, our lives changed. My grandfather was not in good health and I could see it was getting worse. I saw his tears, I felt his pain. Those were terrible days. We found ourselves lying about his health to my uncles and my aunt, because we didn't want them to come back to Iraq since they might be in very serious danger. Just the idea that a person has come back to Iraq from another country can be enough to get them kidnapped or killed. They were hard days, when my grandpa wanted to see his children, and his children wanted to see him, and neither could get what they wanted.

My grandpa died after about six months and my grandma refused to leave our house until last month, when she decided to go and see her own child by herself, and stay there. Now, I accept the idea of living without my grandma since she's with her children again. I want her to be happy; I don't want to see her tears anymore.

Now thinking about Baghdad and the family I had there causes me pain. I can't imagine myself there; I don't think I can visit Baghdad without my grandpa, without the family. Seeing the houses without their people is my idea of disaster.

I would pay you with my life if you could just remove this war from history. I thought I was going to study in one of Baghdad's colleges, marry, and have a child that my grandpa would see and love. I was wrong. That's just one dream of many that the war killed.

As you know, your aunts and uncles certainly aren't alone in leaving Iraq; according to the United Nations, since the invasion of Iraq, at least two million Iraqis have fled the country (an additional two million or more are internally displaced). You and your immediate family have stayed in Mosul. Why is this? Do you plan to stay in Iraq?

It would be hard to leave everything you have worked so hard and long to build, and start again from zero. My parents are not young anymore—my dad is about sixty. Would he find a job? I can't say that he would.

Plus, we are Muslims, and this is one thing I'm really proud of. Personally, I couldn't get rid of my hijab (Muslim headscarf); I consider it a crown over my head. I want to be around people who respect these beliefs, and I've heard from friends that in Europe and other countries, they don't treat Arab people, especially Muslims, well. They look at them like they're terrorists, like they are people lower than themselves!

For me, I can't stand this kind of racism. I believe that we are all equal under the law of nature; no one is better than another in anything but what he or she gives. And everyone has the right to choose the religion he believes is the right one.

For the future, I can't make any plans. This is the case for all Iraqis: we live with no plan in mind, because there's no plan we can count on carrying out.

Do you consider your experience typical among Iraqis? Are there ways in which you're better or worse off than the average Iraqi?

In the eyes of most Iraqis, I think I would be an ordinary girl. It's strange for me, or my parents, to see it that way because we see what's unique about me...my dreams, my hobbies.... But if you think about it, everyone is unique, and everyone is precious.

So in other words, I am a normal person and a normal Iraqi, but I am not the standard model!!!

I guess I'm just a little bit better off than average.

What is your greatest hope for your own life and future?

I have a long list of wishes:

1. I want to publish this book.
2. I want to travel around the world.
3. I want to improve my drawing skill.
4. I want to learn to drive a car.
5. I want to learn to play violin.
6. I want to graduate from college with a high average.
7. I want to have a pharmacy of my own.
8. I want to have a big bookshop.
9. I want to marry a great man, and have a great family.

What is your greatest hope for Iraq?

1. I wish for all Iraqis to have both electricity and clean water all day long.
2. I want every Iraqi to have peace in life and peace of mind as well.
3. I want to have a leader that I will be proud of.

Is there anything that makes you feel especially hopeful these days?

Um, I finished my midterm exams today, does that count?

In your blog, you report several different feelings about Saddam Hussein. You first write that before the war, you hated him, and now feel nothing toward him. Later, when he is scheduled to be executed, you say that the Americans "made you love him." What did you mean by this, and what is your opinion today?

It's true that in Saddam's time, we didn't have electricity; the same is true now. But we also didn't have daily explosions, kidnappings, and killings.

The cost of living was more acceptable then. For example, in Saddam's time, the price of gasoline was 5 dinar a day, and now it's 450 dinar. So imagine!! We didn't have Internet connections in Iraq then, we didn't have satellite; we were isolated from the world around us. The salaries were low. But on the other hand, we had rations given to every family every month.

So, Saddam didn't hurt me personally, but I think this war did. This war hurt everyone personally. This war turned our lives upside down. No plans can be settled because nothing goes as expected.

For example, the night before my exams, I study when the electricity turns on and stop when it turns off. I feel like a machine running on the electricity supply. I use a battery light when I can, and when the battery's low, I'm low. When it turns off, I switch off and go to sleep.

There's an old Moslawi women's saying: "The crazy person you know is better than the sane person you don't know."

In the United States, some people think that the occupation should end right away. Others think that U.S. troops need to stay. What do you think?

Something I learned over the years: nothing goes as expected. I feel like I'm lost, like I don't know the right thing. I don't know who I should believe when I'm surrounded by so many liars.

Your family is Sunni, but you rarely write about this on the blog, although you write often of your Muslim faith. What do you think about the sectarian violence in Iraq? Is it something you experienced before the war, and why do you think it has become more pronounced over the last several years?

Before the war, no one asked for others' religion. Take me as an example, I didn't know the difference between Sunni and Shia! Maybe I was just ignorant of these issues, but believe me, others who were more aware of this didn't care. The war created this moment, when we would be judged according to our religion and faith. I think we are all Iraqi, we were and will always be *only Iraqi*.

One of my relatives is married to a Shiite, and we were and we still are okay with this. There's no wrong unless you make it wrong!

Do you think divisions between Sunnis, Shia, and Kurds can be overcome, and if so, how?

Yes, I think it only needs time. I don't know how, but I have a strong belief in this because in the end, we are all Iraqi. And this country will always be ours, no matter what!

What would you tell Barack Obama about Iraq?

I want to say to Obama: If you can't get things back to the way it was, if you can't compensate for all the damage that has happened to my country, then please at least stop the damaging.

Someone said, "Handsome is as handsome does." Occupying other countries is not handsome behavior.

From my point of view: The greatest men are not those who are so valued by the people of their country that they become leaders but are those who leave their position still being valued highly by all peoples.

Last words to end my letter:

Be gentle with the Iraqi.

Additional Materials

August 3, 2006

"In my Wonderland we would have electricity and clear water"

American students interview Hadiya*

We are a group of students attending the Asheville School's summer academic program. As part of our class we contacted a girl living in Iraq. Hadiya, as she prefers to be called, is a seventeen-year-old living in Mosul who writes about her life in her online blog, iraqigirl.blogspot.com. We were able to discover a new perspective on the war in Iraq by reading her blog. We then each emailed her a question.

MY NAME IS ALEX and I am from the suburbs of Washington, D.C. I am fifteen years old. In your post you mention the story *Alice in Wonderland*. This is one of my favorite books and when I was younger, I often daydreamed about traveling to my own version of

* Reprinted with permission from the Asheville Global Report.

Wonderland. If you were to fall down the rabbit's hole, as Alice did, what would your Wonderland be like?

Hadiya: The most beautiful thing in my Wonderland [would be] that we [would] have both electricity and clear water all the time.... All the people in my Wonderland [would] feel in peace because they [would] live in peace. Anyway, I don't dream so much because I know it's hard to live my imagination; but it's really helpful to lie [to] yourself and pretend that you live in your own Wonderland....

MY NAME IS GEORGE BOSTON. I'm fifteen years old and I live in Brooklyn, New York. I know that if there was a war going on around me it would be difficult for me to fall asleep knowing that the next day may be my last. How hard is it for you to fall asleep at night?

Hadiya: It's too easy to fall asleep and it's too easy to wake up. Since the situation became so bad, it's become easy to fall asleep because it's the only way to run from reality. And I think it's easier and better for my health to know that tomorrow would be my last day because I don't live the life. I want to live the life but I can't find it.

MY NAME IS KAYLA and I am fifteen years of age. I live in Atlanta, Georgia. Being that all of the turmoil is going on between my country and yours, I often wonder how things would be different if I was in a position of power. If you had a chance to be in a position of power or a leadership role in your country, what would it be and what would you do differently as a leader?

Hadiya: I am [an] Iraqi and I live in Iraq, but I still don't know what is going on. Who is right? Who is wrong? Who is my enemy? Who is my leader? I don't want to be a leader. But if I was a leader, I [would] ask [the] American government to take their soldiers to their own country where they need to be. The situation gradually became worse day after day since they arrived to Iraq. Their famil[ies] need them more than we do. In fact, we don't need them at all.

MY NAME IS HASTING BUTLER. I'm sixteen years old and I'm from Atlanta, Georgia. I have gained some knowledge of your lifestyle. I want to show you compassion and heart, even when Americans seem least likely to have it. I understand the nights of endless crying, the times you wish you could leave, and the days you feel so depressed, you don't want live. It's not fair for you or anybody to suffer like this. On your seventeenth birthday, you smiled. You said you feel guilty when you smile because it's not right, in your belief, to smile after so many families have been destroyed. Personally, I can partially agree with this, seeing families randomly and unfairly destroyed would make me upset, yet I still don't really understand because I haven't been in a situation like yours. Does this mean you must live in sadness eternally?

Hadiya: You want to feel my pain.... It's not hard to feel my pain. But it's hard to write about my pain, it's hard to translate the feeling into words; they are not from the same type. Words are just words; you read [them] and [they] just pass in your heart. But the feelings are leaving...steps on your heart.

It [hurts] to see your age pass and all the power you have to change your life die. And that just because you are living in Iraq....

[Do you want to know] if I wasn't liv[ing] in Iraq, [what] my life would look like? Would I be happy? Would I be someone?

Sometimes in life you feel your life is over but someone came to you and help[ed] you to draw a smile in your face, help[ed] you to feel joy you didn't feel before. This someone for me was my niece Aya. Sometimes in life you feel your life is over but suddenly you're shocked that there is someone just like Aya; her life is just beginning to start and [it's] over at the same time.

She doesn't know her grandpa because someone from [the] USA killed him.... She's my niece...my only hope and my only [depression].

MY NAME IS VERA and I live in Moscow, Russia. I've just graduated from high school and entered the Moscow Linguistic Academy. Russia is one of the biggest countries in the world and we know about what is happening in Iraq now; not everything, just the things they speak about in the evening news. But you are a person who lives there and knows everything from the inside. Do you think that the countries of the Middle East will be able to maintain their own governments? Do you think they will be independent in the future?

Hadiya: You can call me a [pessimistic] person because I think there is no hope in Iraq. The news you [have] heard covered a little. Some days passed and all [of] Mosul was in a very bad situation. People dying here and...cars exploded and the news channel[s] don't mention anything at all. The life we live is too bad and too dangerous but the life in Baghdad is worse. They said it can't be worse and the next day our relatives called and said it became worse. I [cried] every day before I went to bed; I missed my grandpa and my grandma (they are living in Baghdad); I didn't see them for a long time and I feel I will not see them ever again.

MY NAME IS CHERRY MENG, and I am an international student from China. I was still in China when the Iraq War started, so, I have a unique view on the whole event. I want to show my strongest compassion for you and I want to give you my sincere support. After reading your blog, I personally think you have tasted bitterness, while I can still sense your thirst for sweetness. You have a closer relationship than others with your parents and friends, and even us because of your blog. I truly admire the way you express yourself, but I wonder, meanwhile, do you feel lonely in your world?

Hadiya: I am really close to my parents and my friends somehow. But I certainly feel lonely sometimes. I mean sometimes I feel that nobody understands me or nobody cares about me but I think all...teenager[s] feel that sometimes, [don't] they? I think this is the only [thing] I shared with...teenagers in your place. I think...teenager[s] in Iraq [are] more calm and quiet than teenager[s] in your country. But yes, they feel lonely sometimes, especially [when] they can't go out of their house because of the curfew and the bad situation. This help[s] them somehow to build a good relationship with their parents.

I AM BELLA NUNEZ and I just turned sixteen. I live in Houston, Texas, but my parents are from Mexico. Reading how you have suffered and try to survive in Iraq makes me appreciate everything around me. Like everyone I wanted to see my county rise again after September 11, 2001, just like you want to see Iraq rise as well. I want to know what it would look like for Iraq to "rise again?" I want to let you know that I admire you but, if you are not happy in Iraq, find happiness somewhere else. Stay strong and do not let anyone break you down.

Hadiya: First of all, I can't leave Iraq; I can't live in a foreign country without my parents. And we can't find a job for my parents.... I just want to ask you something. After September 11 took place, what did you feel? Do you feel in pain? I feel this every day. It's only a building destroyed...five years [ago] and you still remember that pain and that suffering. Well, for me it was not one building, it was a country and it's still under the occupation.

And every day one thousand people die. Do you think I will forget this? I can't.... If I live [to] be one hundred years old, maybe I will forget my name and my country, but I will never forget the pain and suffering I am feeling right now.

Sorry if I talk so much. But every time someone talks about September 11 I become angry because I know that he (or she) doesn't have any tiny idea about what is going on [here].

MY NAME IS ANDREW DOS SANTOS, I am sixteen years old. I go to boarding school in North Carolina, but my home is in New

York City. I am dark enough to be considered African American, but my parents are from Brazil and I am sure my roots go back to Africa. Motivation comes to me from my father and mother; they are what keep me going, and my faith. What keeps you from giving up and how do you maintain hope?

Hadiya: Why did you [mention] you are black? Is that important for you?

One of the things we don't do in the Middle East, we don't care about the human color.... One of the Prophet's orders is not [to discriminate] between the people because they are rich or poor, from a famous family or not, black or white, etc.

I [give] up sometimes...when I wake up in the morning [to] the sound of bomb. I feel like...someone took my heart and returned it back to my body.... Just like the computer...if you are working and it's suddenly turned off, you might lose the file you work on but you still have the last file. Can you understand my view?

Discussion Questions

1. Hadiya's sister, father, uncle, and several other family members all blog as well. Why do you think so many members of her family blog about their experiences of the war? Why do you think they all blog in English? Do you have a blog? In Hadiya's situation, do you think you would?

2. What do you think this blog's readership might be like? What are the reasons people in the United States might read this blog? In other countries? Would people you know read a blog like this? Where does your information about Iraq usually come from?

3. Several other young people's wartime diaries have become famous testaments of the experience of war—Anne Frank's Holocaust diary and Zlata Filipovic's diary from Sarajevo, for

example. This book is based not on a personal diary, but on a blog. How do you think writing for an audience might have affected what Hadiya wrote?

4. Hadiya several times reports negative experiences with U.S. soldiers and expresses anger at their presence in Iraq. She also says that she respects the American people and that her family has had positive feelings for U.S. soldiers in the past, and some U.S. military family members comment positively on her blog. What do you think her overall attitude to Americans is? To soldiers? How do you think U.S. soldiers would react to her blog?

5. When Hadiya discusses the unsanitary conditions at her school (on February 2, 2005), some American blog readers plan to contact the Minister of Education to fix the problem. Hadiya is pessimistic that it will work. Why do you think they have such different reactions?

6. In some places, Hadiya responds to comments, both positive and negative, from blog readers. How do you think this dialogue might affect her ideas about Americans?

7. Hadiya repeatedly says she will stop blogging about politics, but always returns to her opinions about the war. Why do you think she repeatedly makes this vow, and why does she keep seeming to change her mind?

8. Hadiya talks about several journalists kidnapped, in Iraq and in Colombia. She says (on February 13, 2005) she has read all 1,800 messages of support for kidnapped journalist Florence Aubenas. Why do you think this is important to her? Are there world events that feel personally significant to you?

9. Hadiya reports several different feelings about Saddam Hussein. She repeatedly says that she has never supported him, but says her opinion of him changes when he is captured. Why do you think this is?

10. Before you read the book, did you have an idea about what life in Iraq would be like? Were there things in Hadiya's story that surprised you? Hadiya is a Sunni Muslim in Mosul, a girl, and, now, a college student; how do you think these facts affect her experience? In what ways do you imagine her experience of occupied Iraq is typical or atypical?

11. In one of her chats with Sasha (November 24, 2006), Hadiya says that the war has changed her, but not all for the bad. What do you think she means? Can you see changes in her over the course of the book?

12. Shortly after starting her blog (on December 9, 2004), Hadiya writes that she wants to do something for Iraq, with its people, but she is not sure what to do. Four years later, after she has started college (as she states in the Afterword), she praises her fellow students' determination to do something, mentioning demonstrations and philanthropic work. Do you think she has a clearer idea now of what she wants to do, or not? What do you think you would do if you were in Iraq?

13. What do you think should happen in Iraq? Do you think the U.S. occupation should end? Do you think Hadiya would agree? Do you think most Iraqis would?

Timeline

Throughout the years Hadiya has been blogging, Mosul has been a center of insurgency against the U.S. occupation. Violence rages literally daily in Iraq, and occurs frequently, from all sides, in Mosul.

This timeline does not aim to comprehensively describe either events in Iraq or events that happened in Hadiya's immediate vicinity. Thus, gaps in the timeline should not be taken to reflect calm—only an absence of events that can be well summarized in brief.

Rather, this timeline lists some of the most important events in Iraq as a whole, in Mosul, and in Hadiya's life, to help readers place Hadiya's story in a broader narrative of the war, and to understand what was—and is—happening around her.

2003

MARCH 19   The U.S. war on Iraq begins.

APRIL 9   Baghdad falls to the United States.

MAY 1   Speaking in front of a "Mission Accomplished" banner, George W. Bush declares that "Major combat operations in Iraq have ended."

DECEMBER 14   The United States captures Saddam Hussein on a farm near Tikrit.

2004

JANUARY 28   Chief U.S. arms investigator David Kay tells the U.S. Congress that no weapons of mass destruction were found in Iraq. "Our intelligence got it all wrong."

MARCH 31–
APRIL 29   After four U.S. contractors with the Blackwater Corporation are killed and displayed by insurgents in Fallujah, the U.S. launches large-scale attacks in that city and in Najaf. In a major defeat, U.S. Marines are ultimately expelled from Fallujah by insurgent Iraqi forces.

APRIL 28   CBS airs photos revealing torture by U.S. soldiers of prisoners at the Abu Ghraib prison outside Baghdad, sparking a worldwide scandal.

MAY 28   One month before the United States is to formally turn over power to an interim government, Iyad Allawi, a secular Shiaa, is chosen as interim prime minister. He is chosen by the Iraqi Governing Council, a body serving under the U.S.-led Coalition Provisional Authority (CPA), and serves as prime minister of Iraq until April 7, 2005.

JUNE 3   Hadiya, not yet blogging, turns fifteen.

JUNE 7   United Nations Resolution 1546 declares the legitimacy of the government in Iraq led by Iyad Allawi.

JUNE 24   On the eve of the installation of Allawi's interim government, coordinated insurgent attacks occur all over Iraq, including car bombs killing sixty-two people in Mosul, where Hadiya lives.

JUNE 28   In an early morning surprise ceremony two days before the announced date, the U.S.-led Coalition Provisional Authority hands over sovereignty to the interim government led by Iyad Allawi. L. Paul Bremer, head of the CPA, leaves Iraq.

JULY 29   Hadiya begins her IraqiGirl blog.

AUGUST 3   Dozens of masked militants fight running gun battles with U.S. troops in Mosul.

AUGUST 20   Sérgio Viera de Mello, the UN Secretary General's Special Representative in Iraq, is among those killed by a car bomb attack in Baghdad. After a second bombing at the UN headquarters in Iraq one month later, Kofi Annan, then the Secretary General of the UN, withdraws most UN staff from Iraq.

AUGUST 22 U.S. planes bomb the Imam Ali mosque in Najaf, the holiest Shiaa shrine, taking out an ancient minaret.

SEPTEMBER 1 Hadiya's niece Aya is born.

OCTOBER 28 A preliminary study of Iraqi households by the British journal *The Lancet* reveals that one hundred thousand more Iraqis died during the first eighteen months of the war than would likely have died otherwise.

NOVEMBER 2 George W. Bush is reelected as U.S. president.

NOVEMBER 6– NOVEMBER 8 Ten thousand U.S. troops amass at Fallujah, joined by more arriving from Mosul, and begin a full-scale assault. Insurgents flow in the opposite direction, leaving Fallujah for Mosul and setting the stage for what will come to be known as the "Battle of Mosul" in the coming weeks. Later, the United States admits to having used the illegal weapon white phosphorus, which burns through skin to the bone, in Fallujah.

NOVEMBER 11 Insurgents take five police stations in Mosul and distribute weapons in solidarity with Fallujah. Aya's grandfather is killed by U.S. gunfire.

NOVEMBER 13–

NOVEMBER 18   U.S. forces are evicted from Saddam Hussein's palace in Mosul. The next day, the governor's house in Mosul is burned to the ground. With two thirds of the city under rebel control, U.S. infantry units that had been dispatched to Fallujah are sent back to Mosul to quell the rebellion, occupying the city in the coming days. Although casualty figures for the Battle of Mosul are unofficial, at least two hundred people are estimated to have died. In Fallujah, at least ten thousand homes were destroyed, and many former residents have never returned.

DECEMBER 30   All seven hundred employees of the Mosul Election Commission resign en masse after receiving death threats. The commission had been appointed in advance of the planned January 30, 2005, elections, the first elections held in U.S.-occupied Iraq.

As 2005 dawns, an Al-Jazeera poll shows that 82 percent of Sunni Iraqis and 69 percent of Shia Iraqis favor immediate U.S. withdrawal.

2005

JANUARY 5   French journalist Florence Aubenas is abducted in Baghdad. Hadiya blogs about it on February 13.

JANUARY 19   A wave of car bombings hits Baghdad, shortly after Hadiya's visit.

JANUARY 30 Iraqis vote for a new interim parliament, amid attacks at polling places. In Mosul, an estimated fifteen thousand people are kept from casting a ballot by sectarian violence.

FEBRUARY 5 Hadiya's school resumes for the spring term. Three days later, it will close due to flooding, and she will be moved to a new school with sixty-student classes.

APRIL 9 Tens of thousands of Shias march to Firdos Square on the second anniversary of the famous toppling of the Saddam Hussein statue there, to demand an end to the U.S. occupation.

END OF APRIL Hadiya visits Baghdad.

MAY 6 Hadiya gets her Iraqi citizenship.

JUNE 3 Hadiya turns sixteen.

LATE JULY The Iraqi blogger Khalid is arrested, then ultimately released. Hadiya blogs about his arrest on July 20.

AUGUST 6 Kurds demand an autonomous state under the new constitution.

MID-AUGUST Hadiya travels to Syria and Jordan.

AUGUST 31 A huge Shia religious procession crossing the al-Aima Bridge over the Tigris River panics at rumors of an insurgent attack. As many as one thousand people may have died.

OCTOBER 15   Iraqis vote for a new constitution.

DECEMBER 15   A 67 percent turnout is claimed in parliamentary elections. Sunnis vote in big numbers but, as in the last elections, Shias win a near absolute majority. Large-scale demonstrations rigged elections follow over the next several weeks.

DECEMBER 19   Violent demonstrations break out all over Iraq as gasoline and cooking fuel prices soar 900 percent.

DECEMBER 25   Mosul, which has a substantial Christian population, sees Christmas Day sectarian bombings targeting Christians.

2006

FEBRUARY 14   Doctors in Mosul demonstrate publicly, stating that that they are subject to extortion, kidnapping, and murder; denouncing the exit fees charged to leave Iraq; and threatening civil disobedience if their security situation does not improve. According to the Association of Muslim Scholars, three hundred professionals have been assassinated in Iraq since the war began. Hadiya's father is a doctor in Mosul.

FEBRUARY 22   Sunni insurgents dressed as police blow up the Golden Dome of the Askaryah Shrine in Samarrah, one of the most sacred sites of Shia worship. This bombing becomes a significant turning point in Iraqi history as reprisals against Sunni mosques follow immediately, plunging Iraq into a new phase of sectarian warfare.

MARCH 5   The *Mosul Observer* reports that U.S. soldiers stopped a bus full of women students from the Teachers' Institute and forced them to remove their hijabs. The soldiers are accused of touching the womens' breasts. When the students protest, forty of them are arrested, triggering confrontations in the city.

MARCH 8   Five civilians are killed by U.S. fire in Mosul, including a child, a pregnant woman, and Hadiya's father's uncle.

MARCH 9   Hadiya's school is hit by mortar fire.

MARCH 26   Sectarian slaughter continues; nationally, 151 die in two days of violence. In Mosul, the governor, a Kurd, narrowly escapes an assassination attempt, and a high school student evades a similar fate by throwing himself into the Tigris.

APRIL 4   Saddam Hussein and six co-defendants are charged with genocide for poison gas attacks on Kurds in the late 1980s.

APRIL 22   Nouri al-Maliki, with U.S. support, takes over from Ibrahim al-Jaafari as prime minister of Iraq.

APRIL 25   The Oil Ministry in Mosul, which has been withholding oil shipments without explanation, releases forty tankers to resupply the city's gas stations.

APRIL 29   The Iraqi Red Crescent estimates that one hundred thousand have fled their homes since the Golden Dome bombing two months earlier. Around this time, Hadiya's father goes to France for one month.

MAY 3   The Iraqi government's Sunni delegation refuses to take its seats in parliament due to stepped-up Shia attacks. Meanwhile, Hadiya's nephew Ayman is born.

JUNE 3   Hadiya turns seventeen.

JUNE 7   The U.S. drops five hundred bombs on a farmhouse in Diyala, purportedly killing Al Qaeda in Mesopotamia leader Abu Musab al-Zarqawi.

      Elsewhere, three students are assassinated on their way to classes at Mosul University, where Hadiya's sister Najma takes classes.

JUNE 15   The U.S. death toll in Iraq reaches 2,500.

JUNE 24   Iraqi agencies calculate that fifty thousand Iraqis have died since 2003. The U.S. military, which claims to keep no count, says the number is no more than thirty thousand. A Johns Hopkins University professor's extrapolation of the British *Lancet* study estimates that up to 660,000 Iraqis have been killed thus far in the war.

      Around this time, Hadiya begins her correspondence with humanitarian relief worker Sasha Crow.

JULY 3   Four U.S. troops and one recently discharged soldier are charged in the rape-murder of fourteen-year-old Abeer Cassim al-Janabi, and the massacre of her family, in Haditha on March 11.

JULY The sectarian bloodshed continues. 3,600 Iraqis died in the July violence all over Iraq, 1,500 of them in Baghdad. 162,000 refugees have by this time registered with the government.

SEPTEMBER 6 Hadiya visits Syria again, as the Iraqi Parliament extends an ongoing state of emergency for thirty more days.

SEPTEMBER 10 The U.S. military arrests an eight-year-old girl in south Mosul. According to the *Mosul Observer*, district residents, including local police, gather and take over the building where she is being held to force her release. The governor of Ninevah, Duraid Kashmoula, intervenes and the girl is released by the United States eighteen hours after her arrest.

SEPTEMBER 27 Patrick Cockburn, writing in the British newspaper the *Guardian*, calculates that seventy thousand Kurds have fled Mosul in recent months. Forty to fifty civilians are being killed in that northern city, where Hadiya lives, every week.

NOVEMBER 8 In the United States, Democrats narrowly win a majority in Congress; the vote is widely seen as a rejection of then-president George W. Bush's war policies. In Baghdad, the Iraqi Parliament extends the state of emergency another thirty days. It will be extended again on November 28.

NOVEMBER 24   Hadiya's friend Haneen leaves Iraq for Canada.

DECEMBER 13   The Syrian government estimates that eight hundred thousand Iraqi refugees are now living in Syria, mostly in and around Damascus, the capital.

DECEMBER 30   Saddam Hussein is executed by hanging on the first day of Eid, the Muslim religious holiday.

DECEMBER 31   Saddam Hussein is buried in his hometown of Ouja near Tikrit. The death toll for U.S. soldiers in Iraq reaches three thousand.

2007

JANUARY   The United States begins a troop "surge," sending twenty thousand more troops into Iraq and extending the tour of duty of some additional troops.

JANUARY 13   Ninevah governor Duraid Kashmoula's car is searched by U.S. troops outside the Mosul Sports Ministry. Local athletes stage a sit-in to protest.

JANUARY 24   The Student & Youth Union at Mosul University stages a march to protest arrest, by U.S. forces, of six students.

FEBRUARY 15   Three members of the Mosul University Student & Youth Union are arrested by U.S. troops. Meanwhile, a U.S. audit reveals that $10 billion in military contracts is not accounted for.

FEBRUARY 16   The number of bodies dumped in Baghdad daily plunges from forty to fifty per day to just ten; the success is attributed by the United States to the "surge" in troop deployments.

MARCH 5   The famous book market on Baghdad's Mutanabi Street is bombed, with thirty-eight Iraqis killed. The UN announces it will open a refugee office in Amman, Jordan. Since the war began, 3.6 million Iraqis have fled their homes, most since the Golden Dome bombing. 1.8 million have left Iraq and the other 1.8 million are internally displaced.

APRIL 1   Six hundred Iraqis have been killed in sectarian violence in the past week. An Iraqi military spokesperson says that the security sweep of Baghdad is driving insurgents north to Mosul, where gunmen have taken over the telephone exchange.

APRIL 9   Tens of thousands of Iraqis, many wrapped in the Iraqi flag, march from Kufa to Najaf on the fourth anniversary of the fall of Baghdad, protesting the U.S. occupation.

APRIL 16   The United States announces that it now holds eighteen thousand Iraqi prisoners.

MAY 3   Sixty-four bodies have been found in Mosul in the past week. Authorities count 23 mortar attacks, 29 explosions, and 23 armed clashes. During April, Mosul suffered 244 homicides, 137 explosions, 123 armed incidents, and 93 armed clashes. The numbers reflect the movement of insurgents to Mosul from Anbar and Baghdad due to the U.S. troop surge.

MAY 16   Coordinated insurgent attacks take place across Mosul, targeting bridges, police stations, and prisons; the city is put on total curfew. Iraqi security forces repel many of the attacks, but the Badoush Bridge is destroyed. The United States claims the day as a victory for the U.S.-trained Iraqi security, evincing progress in the occupation.

MAY 17   Nine mortar rounds hit the U.S. embassy, the second attack on the U.S. "Green Zone" in two days. Meanwhile, U.S. and Iraqi troops arrest three hundred in Mosul, following on the previous day's attacks. Some Iraqis are critical of the U.S. military's response. According to the *Mosul Observer*, "The U.S. army shot Kamal Abdul Baqi, an 83-year-old retired teacher, for refusing to let their guard dogs into his home. Mr. Abdul Baqi is both blind and deaf."

MAY   Hadiya's grandfather dies.

JUNE 23   The UN estimates that 2.2 million Iraqis have fled their country since the war began.

JULY   Hadiya takes her college entrance exams, after they are postponed three times.

JULY 30   Jordan pleads for international help as nearly a million Iraqi refugees flee across its borders. Relief agencies report that eight million Iraqis, mostly children, are at risk from hunger, inadequate medical attention, or lack of housing.

JULY 31   The U.S. Government Accounting Office cannot account for 190,000 weapons destined for Iraqi security forces in 2004–2005.

AUGUST   Hadiya gets her college exam scores and decides to attend the College of Pharmacy.

AUGUST 15   In a sectarian attack, Mosul's Kurdish National Union is hit by car bombs.

AUGUST 16   Five bridges in Mosul are closed after clashes in surrounding neighborhoods. Hadiya's father witnesses a doctor being kidnapped near his clinic and alerts the *Mosul Observer*.

AUGUST 31   Cholera hits north of Iraq, killing ten. 3,737 U.S. troops have died in combat in Iraq by the end of August, putting 2007 on track to become the highest casualty year for the Americans to date. 1,809 Iraqi civilians were killed throughout Iraq during the month, with 1,760 having died in July. Meanwhile, General David Petraeus says Bush's troop surge is working.

SEPTEMBER 3   George W. Bush pays a surprise visit to al-Assad Air Force base, outside Baghdad, to impress upon the U.S. Congress that his troop surge is working. The British withdraw their last troops from Basra.

SEPTEMBER 11 Health officials report more than seven thousand cases of cholera throughout Iraq.

SEPTEMBER 28 Iraqi Prime Minister Nouri al-Maliki upbraids the U.S. Senate for pushing a plan to partition Iraqi in Kurdish, Sunni, and Shia states.

OCTOBER 1 On the first day of the fall school term, Mosul University is attacked and a professor of agriculture is killed. Hadiya's cousin is injured by the bomb blast.

OCTOBER 30 The U.S. Army Corps of Engineers announces that the Mosul Dam is in danger of collapsing, a catastrophe that would destroy Mosul and bring devastation all the way to Baghdad. The Iraqi government disputes that the dam is in danger of collapse.

NOVEMBER 8 Five hundred prisoners are released by the U.S. military. The U.S. is holding twenty-nine thousand Iraqis in prisons.

DECEMBER 16 British forces turn over the last province under their control in southern Iraq. 174 British troops have died during the U.S. and British occupation. The cost to British taxpayers has been equivalent to ten billion U.S. dollars. Meanwhile, Turkish planes attack Iraqi Kurdish villages and claim to kill 150 "rebels."

Publisher's Acknowledgments

Haymarket Books would like to gratefully acknowledge the efforts of Sasha Crow of the Collateral Repair Project, whose contributions to this book's publication are too many and too varied to enumerate individually.

We received helpful advice and assistance from Tessa Michaelson and others at the University of Wisconsin-Madison's Cooperative Children's Book Center, from Marc Aronson of the *School Library Journal*'s Nonfiction Matters blog, and from Emily Goldstein.

We would also like to acknowledge Tanya Buckingham and the student workers at the University of Wisconsin-Madison's Cartography Lab, who made the maps included in the book, and Ameed Saabneh for Arabic assistance. Finally, we would like to thank the *Asheville Global Report* for permission to use their interview with Hadiya, and Hossam H. for permission to use his picture of Mecca.

Hadiya's blog is online at http://iraqigirl.blogspot.com

About Haymarket Books

Haymarket Books is a nonprofit, progressive book distributor and publisher, a project of the Center for Economic Research and Social Change. We believe that activists need to take ideas, history, and politics into the many struggles for social justice today. Learning the lessons of past victories, as well as defeats, can arm a new generation of fighters for a better world. As Karl Marx said, "The philosophers have merely interpreted the world; the point, however, is to change it."

We take inspiration and courage from our namesakes, the Haymarket Martyrs, who gave their lives fighting for a better world. Their 1886 struggle for the eight-hour day, which gave us May Day, the international workers' holiday, reminds workers around the world that ordinary people can organize and struggle for their own liberation. These struggles continue today across the globe—struggles against oppression, exploitation, hunger, and poverty.

It was August Spies, one of the Martyrs targeted for being an immigrant and an anarchist, who predicted the battles being fought to this day. "If you think that by hanging us you can stamp out the labor movement," Spies told the judge, "then hang us. Here you will tread upon a spark, but here, and there, and behind you, and in front of you, and everywhere, the flames will blaze up. It is a subterranean fire. You cannot put it out. The ground is on fire upon which you stand."

We could not succeed in our publishing efforts without the generous financial support of our readers. Many people contribute to our project through the Haymarket Sustainers program, where donors receive free books in return for their monetary support. If you would like to be a part of this program, please contact us at info@haymarketbooks.org.

Shop our full catalog of books for changing the world online at www.haymarketbooks.org or call 773-583-7884.